THE ROAD IS AN UNFINISHED SONG

A true story of selling up, buying
a van and following a dream

Adam Piggott

To Yvonne
with love
Best wishes

CONTENTS

For Jayne, I said I'd write you a song

1. YOU DID WHAT?

I glanced behind me into the back of the van we bought this morning. There they are, all our worldly belongings piled too high and in no particular order. Jayne and I driving, feels more like racing up the A12 into Essex. Not a good road to contemplate whether we've started living the dream or have just made the biggest mistake of our lives. A fast dual carriageway, catapulting traffic out of London, white vans and lorries overtaking us in both lanes, pushing us ahead. Pushing us into the dragnet of speed cameras that want to slow us down, speed cameras that don't seem to apply to anyone else. Pushing, pulling, accelerating, braking, maybe it's all trying to tell us something. Maybe it's a sign of the perils and pitfalls of choosing to sell our home and start living a life on the road.

Neither of us has said anything for a while, silent inside the front of the van compared to the rush hour going on around us. This is what we've been waiting over a year for. The dream of selling our flat, cutting our costs and going on a journey with our music. Jayne and I writing songs, doing pub, bar and restaurant gigs, busking on the side if we need to. What are we doing? A middle-aged husband and wife trying to make a living playing music.

Don't ask about the fine detail, there isn't any, there never has been and it didn't take long to realise there never could be. We'd shied away from telling anyone at first, we knew what the questions would be, we knew we couldn't answer them. Having tried to justify it to ourselves, we knew most things remained unanswered.

Actually, we did ask a friend what he thought. We asked Crazy Bob (aka Martini Bob – any time, any place, anywhere). A regular visitor to the casinos of Las Vegas, he'd also once sold up, put everything in a trailer and driven to Spain. Even he had to think about our plan when we told him, he went unusually quiet for a minute. We waited, trying to read his poker face, nervous of how he'd respond to the secret we'd shared. No doubt he was rolling the dice, shuffling the deck and stacking up the odds. His Manchester accent added a daring spin to the answer when he eventually said,

"Gof'r it, what have you got to lose?"

So Bob had come through in the affirmative and we had a seal of approval. A gambler's nod to an unknowable future, untried and untested.

Another lorry overtakes, long and heavy, rolling past until it can pull into the space in front of us. Leaning back in the passenger seat I try to make some more headroom, the top of my head's touching the van roof. Why didn't I think to get in the front seat, try sitting in it before buying it? Jayne's leaning back too, away from the steering wheel, looking in the rear-view mirror, being pressured by a lorry to speed up. Still, she'd rather be behind the wheel, any journey's too much of a roller coaster for her if she isn't driving. In our twenty two years together whenever we get in a car, she drives. Too many experiences with reckless drivers losing control when she was a teenager.

Reckless! Like selling your house, buying a van and hitting the road with no plan B, no backup or nest egg. Well, a plan of sorts, book gigs wherever we can and let an adventure unfold. Maybe we'll get lucky, maybe there's things out there we'll discover if we just get out into the big wide world. This is what we're telling ourselves anyway.

Jayne accelerates, gives in to the pressure from the lorry behind and overtakes the one in front that rolled past a few moments ago,

"It's a good decision."

"I think I should've stayed behind that lorry."

"No, I mean this."

I point my thumb backwards over my shoulder indicating the bigger picture, our life packed in bags behind us. Jayne's focussed on the road, I can normally read her face but right now I can't tell what she's thinking, she's concentrating, the lorry is behind pulling out again, coming up on the outside, the dance of the trucks is about to repeat itself.

Our life in Hastings had started to feel stale, doing the same things, playing the same places.

We'd had a lot of good times but were ready to move on, it wasn't the town, it was us. The feeling began a few years ago when we played at the world's biggest street-music festival. Ten days in Italy, when it finished we didn't want to go home. We wanted to move on somewhere else, another festival, another gig, another anything, anywhere. We had everything with us, we had each other and our instruments, why go home? The only reason seemed to be to cut the grass and pay the bills. So from then on that's all we could think about, what would it be like if we never had to go home, if we didn't even have a home? Round in circles we went, trying to think it through from every angle, was it sane, was it practical, was it possible, the question wouldn't go away. We're getting older, and the older we get the less likely it is that we'd be able to do this, this is our chance, maybe our last chance. So we said let's do it, properly do it, lock, stock and barrel. What we can't take with us we'll let go of, we're not going to put things in storage, we're not saving stuff just in case.

Our home in Hastings went on the market nine months ago and we've been waiting and waiting, endless delays and false hopes trying to sell our small one-bedroom basement flat. The estate agent called it a 'garden flat' so Martini Bob bought us some nice pots and plants to smarten up the outside, help us on our way. Ralph Waldo Emerson said, "Once you make a decision, the universe conspires to make it happen", but the decision to sell up was made ages ago, if anything, the universe had been putting the brakes on, everything going so slow, month after month. We'd had a false start already, earlier in the year, planning gigs in the west country that we had to go and do in our car, it cost us more in accommodation.

Eventually someone made an offer on our flat but then there were more delays until, all of a sudden, the solicitors decided they agreed with each other. Either that or they'd reached the maximum level of fees they'd hoped to get from such a small sale. The date was set to hand over the keys, two weeks to get rid of everything we couldn't take with us, the changeover coming fast and a lot of stuff still had to go. What we hadn't already sold or given away needed to be got rid of. Already we'd put plenty on eBay, done boot sales and trips to charity shops but there was loads left. Our double bed for starters, not to mention a sofa, lamps, desk, fridge, kitchen accessories we couldn't possibly take with us, it all had to go.

What's left is now in the back of the van, jumbled together behind us, I'm sure we don't need all of it, it wants sorting. Duvet, pillows, clothes, my guitar, Jayne's ukulele, our PA, microphone stands. The spare speaker I'm sure we could do without, the oversize blue suitcase looks like we're going on a long-haul holiday, the plastic bags full of odds and ends like we're doing another run to a charity shop.

Still, we're lucky to have a van to put it all in. Acquiring it at the eleventh hour, like a last minute

Indiana Jones-style roll under a closing door. The sale was leaving us with around £10,000, we called a friend of a friend for advice. She'd been selling her VW a while ago so we thought she might know where to look, or what to look out for.

"That's timely," she says, "I took if off the market back then but I'm just looking to sell it now."

Thank you Ralph Waldo Emerson.

We ran through the spec:

1. A white VW transporter, ten years old, 150,000 miles on the clock and a decent service history.
2. Insulated (the owner is an upholsterer and did it herself)
3. Rock 'n' roll bed (a racy term for a seat that turns into a double bed)
4. Sunroof (Jayne's always said if she's going to give up her home then she wants to lay in bed and look up at the stars)
5. Leisure battery for charging a phone and laptop
6. Tail gate (i.e. a rear door that lifts up so you can sit outside underneath if it rains)

Basically, it's a small van, the kind of size your plumbing and heating engineer would turn up in. You can't stand up in it, there's no kitchen, cupboards or shower or anything. She wanted £8,000 for it. We offered £7,500 and she accepted.

Thanks again Mr Emerson.

So it's our first day on the road and we'd picked the van up this morning, the June sky the kind of blue to make us think summer has really begun. I'd dropped the house keys with the estate agent while Jayne drove our old car to the garage to try to sell it back to the guy we'd bought it from.

I picked her up outside the garage, thumbs in her pockets and a cheeky half-smile on her face told me she'd done the deal. With her persuasive powers and him having informed us last year of it's solid reliability he didn't really have an option not to buy it back. Jayne jumped into the driver's seat, I swapped over to the passenger side and tried to ignore the feeling of the top of my head touching the roof. The car was the last item to go, the last connection to our suburban life, it's gone, our house has gone and our home's gone.

We've been booking gigs in various parts of the country based on no particular logic other than who will have us and who will pay us. Is this plan going to work? It has to. Here we are driving to Ipswich for our first one, everything just slung in the back, messy, disorganised, we haven't even put the rock 'n' roll bed up yet.

With all the uncertainty in our life we're staying in a cheap hotel tonight, from now on wherever we are will be our home, no looking back. Mind you, when I do, it reminds me we've still got way too much stuff.

2. SCRAPES

"**W**e had a great ska band here last weekend."

The barman's looking over my shoulder at no one in particular, "They love ska, place was packed."

Ipswich, Sunday afternoon, the pub's quiet, not just quiet, tired too, old shades of burgundy and brown, a world away from the four lanes of traffic going past it's front doors. A couple of old guys are drinking pints at the bar, staring at the cloudy liquid in the glasses in front of them. One of them looks over, says something under his breath, the other picks up his drink in response. Regulars, I know they're not here to listen to us. I can see one of our A4 posters below eye level on the far wall, dust floating in the shafts of light coming through a window that rattles as a large lorry goes by. Jayne and I look at each other, do we know any ska, the thought flashes across my mind. Our music's pretty easy going, Jayne's got a mellow tone to her voice when she sings, plays her own style of fingerstyle ukulele, me on the acoustic guitar, a kind of folk, Americana, world music.

The barman waves us over to a dark area of

the lounge and we put the first of our gear down. Hanging up our coats I turn a light on to brighten up the shadows,

"Can you smell burning?"

Jayne has a point, there's an odour in the air that doesn't smell right. There are cigarette burns on the table, it could be the furniture.

A few trips to the van until our collection of cases, instruments, speakers and mic stands are resting on chairs or lying on the worn out carpet ready to unpack and set up. Is anyone going to be here? There's just the barman and the two old guys at the bar with their backs to us.

The bigger question at this stage of a gig in a pub is whether we get a free drink. We're not looking to get drunk or anything. I don't drink alcohol, I don't like it, I never acquired a taste for it, a few years of peer pressure drinking in my late teens until I realised I didn't have to join in. Jayne likes a drink though, pub gigs don't pay that much so getting one means it's not costing us to be here. Helps us feel welcome, playing to strangers in a strange venue in a strange town. It's a principle thing and there's three ways the hospitality can go:

1. When Jayne made the booking they said we'd each get a couple of free drinks. Best option.

2. The venue didn't mention anything about it but when we arrive they're immediately forthcoming with "What can we get you?" Good option, smiles all round. Some ambiguity as to whether we'll get another one.

3. No mention of drinks on the phone or when we arrive. Worst option.

Option 3 leads to the two of us cajoling each other to go and ask at the bar, usually led by Jayne who develops a thirst not long after we've brought our gear in. Today there's been no mention of a drink, it's my turn to ask, it's mostly my turn. The technique I've developed is to choose a quiet moment, no problem in this case, then casually go and say,

"Hi there, we can't remember whether we get a drink as part of the arrangement?"

Mostly this is successful. It reminds me of a story told too often at family gatherings. When I was a young child I went to spend time with my grandfather at his sweet factory, as soon as I got there I announced,

"If you offer me sweets I'm allowed to say yes."

I cringe telling the story, a hangover from the laughter I remember spreading round the room at my expense, too young to feel anything apart from foolish. Anyway my sweet tooth never matured, a taste for sugar never turned to alcohol.

The barman says we can have a couple of drinks, he asks,

"So you're Jack are you?"

"No, I'm Adam."

"What's with the name Wildwood Jack then?"

I wish I could give him a deep and meaningful answer about the name we've chosen for our duo but there isn't one. I resist saying because it was available and no one else was using it but instead say,

"Oh, you know, it was kind of adventurous... anyway, thanks for the drinks."

We'd come up with the name Cinnamon Jack before Wildwood Jack, bought the web hosting and everything, thought it had a nice warm sound to it until we found out it was a brand of cereal in North America. So Wildwood Jack it was and maybe there's a hint of the spirit of freedom about it.

I carry the drinks over to our dusky corner, the dark smokey smell still hanging in the air where we're setting up. A few people seem to have drifted in, seating themselves at casual intervals around the bar, chairs angled approximately in our direction. As we start, the two old guys slide off their stools and make their way out, my view of their backs replaced by the last streaks of white beer froth clinging to the sides of their empty glasses.

At the end, a repeat booking doesn't seem worth asking about. The barman says as much when he tells us of a musician he knows who does okay busking in the town centre. After packing up Jayne lifts her jacket off the hook on the wall, but it's not a hook, it's a large circular light, the dark shadows suddenly illuminated by the bright orange glow of a bulb, the glass too hot to touch. Her jacket has a new black circle burnt into the back of it. We take our gear out bringing the burning smell with us.

It's not the only scar we pick up in Ipswich

either. Our VW is longer than the car Jayne's used to, the owner had said it takes a while to adjust to the length of it. On a tight corner in a multi-storey car park she catches the side of a concrete pillar and puts a one-foot scrape down the side, scratching off the paint to reveal the grey metal underneath. The first and last time we go into a multi-storey.

A couple of days in and we're bruised and marked already, burns and scrapes, visible signs of living on the road are showing sooner that we'd have thought. Two stripes earned and we're having to turn around and go south again to pick up another one, a compulsory attendance at a speed awareness course. A few weeks before hitting the road we were pulled over by the police, Jayne was driving at 38mph on a 30mph road, a long straight run out of Rye towards Hastings, leading up to a national speed limit sign. Houses set back behind trees on one side, open fields on the other, a perfect speed trap, the police were pulling everyone over, £80 to attend a speed awareness course. Damn.

The open road isn't calling, it's being argumentative, testing our resolve. Driving too fast isn't something we ever think about, Jayne's speed is always below the limit. Well, nearly always. She's more interested in finding out what to do with drivers who are regularly queueing up to overtake us. What to do with the cars and vans pressuring her to go faster, peeking out trying to get past, or worse still, flashing their lights and making those exaggerated French/Italian shrugging gestures with their hands off the wheel.

We arrive at the Football Club where the course is held. The car park wraps around two sides of the pitch, sheltered by trees and a grass verge and we put ourselves out by the edge. Jayne goes into the clubhouse, a few other people are making their way in too, the slow closing of car doors, reluctant footsteps of assorted members of society, normally law abiding citizens unlucky enough to have driven at the wrong speed on the wrong stretch of road on the wrong day.

I know they'll be in there for a couple of hours, I open all the doors and the boot and stand looking at all our belongings. All the bags, carrier bags, suitcases and boxes piled up, our attempt to reduce the stuff in our life down to a necessary and transportable amount. The sun is shining, just some small clouds that aren't big enough to obscure it. I get everything out and put it on the grass, the music gear as well, our PA, our instruments, the spare speaker.

The first thing to go has to be the massive blue long-haul suitcase, it's got most of our clothes in it. Bulky, totally inappropriate, inside is a tangled spaghetti of sleeves and trouser legs, getting anything out messes everything else up, it has to go. Other stuff has to go too or we're just dragging the past with us.

I flatten out the rock 'n' roll seat into it's horizontal position and turn it into a bed, spreading out the duvet in it's faded cover, the pillows in place at the back of the van. The bed looks cosy, familiar, the rest of the stuff I put back in, trying to bring some order to this tiny living space, make it ready for it's debut. We're going to stay in it for the first time tonight. The plan is to drive to Bournemouth seafront, get something to eat, then sleep there. We like Bournemouth, we went there once years ago, liked the town, liked the idea of being by the sea for our inaugural night. The ocean, the beach, the palm trees swaying in the breeze, dreaming our first ever dreams in the back of the van.

By mid-afternoon Jayne's finished the course. She jumps in the driver's seat, looks over her shoulder to see our double bed made up, our stuff a little better organised than when she left it.

"Nice one."

She's impressed. Really I've just done a bloke's version of clearing up, moving things around to create the appearance of tidiness. The course was good she says, they told her how to get rid of vehicles pestering her from behind, pull over and let them pass. We drive down to the coast and test out the theory, many times.

Early evening when we get to Bournemouth, we head to the east where there's a long road by the cliffs overlooking the sea. We pull up beside a row of trees, their low trunks knotted, branches curving upwards, leaning at an easy angle over the road, a view of the ocean and the horizon through the spaces in between.

Later that night as we're walking back, it's breezy, the wind flapping my unbuttoned jacket as we're making our way up the slope to where we've parked. It's then that the reality dawns on us, we're about to sleep in the van on the street for the first time. No longer just casual words, empty words without detail, we're going to lie down under the covers and go to bed on the side of the road. We start feeling self-conscious about it, what if someone sees us climbing into the back of the van? What would happen if we were found out? What if you're not allowed to sleep in it here, or anywhere for that matter?

The trees cast a deep shadow over the cars parked along our stretch of the road, the wind is louder as it blows through the branches and leaves above us. We get in the front seat first so we can think this thing over, pretend we're just normal people sitting in darkness in their vehicle. How do normal people behave when they're in the front seat of a car? What's normal, what does it look like to have no intention of getting in the back and sleeping the night? What sort of question is that? We need to calm down and relax a little.

I volunteer to get in the back and put the curtains up. Once I'm in, I push the side door so it's almost closed,

"Wait, someone's coming."

A man is walking a dog up the street towards

us. I stop what I'm doing, one end of a curtain in my hand, the other attached to the popper in the corner of the window that's holding it in place. There are windows all the way round the back of the van, slightly tinted, I hold still, hoping he doesn't see me or wonder why the door is open a little. The dog pauses, sniffing around the trunk of a tree, the man pulls it on and they walk by. I clip the other end of the curtain in place.

On the other side of the road, set in the middle of an expanse of open lawn, there's a large residential retirement block. Seven storeys high, it towers over us, at least half the lights are on in the flats. I'm convinced the people in the flats are watching us and know what we're up to. We decide to walk up and down the esplanade, compose ourselves before we both jump into the back of the van. The more we walk up and down the more conspicuous we feel, another u-turn, up and down the same short stretch of pavement, if our behaviour wasn't suspicious before, it sure is now. A couple more late-night dog walkers come by, lingering as they pass our section of trees. We walk over to the railing at the edge of the cliff, the sky is a deep midnight blue, down below the light of the moon sparkles on a black sea, the wind is swirling around like it's coming from every direction.

Then there's no one around so we take the chance and spring into the van, slam the side door shut and lock ourselves in. We lie in the dark afraid to speak, eyes wide open, awake with nervous energy. Any minute we're expecting a knock on the window,

"Who's in there?"

"Come out with your hands up."

Silence. Nothing. Still nothing. Slowly we begin to relax until finally we fall asleep.

Early next morning, before the dog walkers arrive, we leave town, drive to Somerset over the steady rise and fall of the Dorset hills.

We'd trawled through local what's on listings in various parts of the country, looking for regular events played by solo or duo acts not too dissimilar to ourselves (not ska bands). In Wellington we found a pub with live music and the email address of a local musician who organised it. The trouble with emails, hardly anyone replies, especially not musicians who are busy hustling to get their own gigs. Jon was an exception, he wrote straight back and it was booked, we get a meal and drinks, they pass a hat round for audience donations and the landlady throws in another £20 or so.

There's a crossroads at the centre of Wellington and everything has to drive through it, skewed slightly so that traffic gets clustered in a bottleneck. When it releases us and we move out from the centre, the shops become houses again. It's impossible to miss the pub, the outside walls covered in a big mural, an underwater fantasy, seaweed and shells at the bottom, dolphins and fish swimming around the windows, oxygen bubbles floating up to the roof. A giant aquarium in the middle of a regular street.

The pub is not as soft on the inside as it appears on the outside. Hard floors, brick walls and big solid wooden tables. Every surface is reflective, sounds bounce their way around the bar, it takes a while to adjust to it as we're playing, the echo that's coming back to us from the opposite wall. There's a small local crowd that come for the music, sitting at the long edges of the tables that are set back in rows like a council meeting. Jon comes along too, as friendly in real life as he is in his emails, looks like Quentin Tarantino wearing musician's clothes, faded jeans and a t-shirt, his hands in the pockets of a worn suit jacket. He's enthusiastic, plays gigs around the area, has tips for other bookings for us and to let him know of any places we can recommend for him, says we can arrange another one here for later in the year.

At the end of the night the landlady empties the dimpled pint jug that's been passed around, converts the collection into notes and adds another one herself. She's cool about us staying overnight in the pub driveway, there's room for us to park next to her car, says she'll leave the back door unlocked for us to use the bathroom. After we've packed up and the last of the voices have faded, the pub lights go off and we're lying in bed in the dark, just an outside light shining through the gaps in the curtains. We're tucked away, hidden, no one would know we were in here.

That gig took an email but the next one, on

the North Devon coast, took a lot of phone calls. Tracking down and speaking to the owner took Jayne ages,

"He's out at the moment."

"He's busy."

"He's on another call."

Then even more calls to agree a date, Jayne's like a terrier, she won't let go, persistent, relentless, a pen held crossways in her mouth like a little bone as she's tapping away at the keyboard. She takes it out when making the call, holds it poised over a scrap of paper, scribbling random bits from the conversation that only she can decipher. Afterwards there's never any idle chat about what might happen, the maybes or possibles. Only when they're in the diary, that's when she says,

"Guess what?"

This one's been worth the effort, he'll pay us well, give us food and accommodation too. We'll have to work for it, it's in Croyde, a holiday and surfers destination, tonight we're the entertainment.

Driving into North Devon there's a deeper roll to the landscape's ups and downs. I'm experimenting with the angle of my seat, adjusting the tilt so it gives my head more clearance. As I'm trying to find the sweet spot of how much I need to lean back, a driver of a T4, just like ours, waves at us. T4's are the choice of van for surfers, further along and another one does the same, then another, lifting a hand off the steering wheel to say hi as we pass by, to acknowledge a togetherness. We've unknowingly joined a club, it feels good, the closer we get to the coast, the more we see of them and the more waving we're doing.

The road rises steadily as we get closer to Croyde, bounded by hedgerows until we're high enough that the gaps reveal a vast sandy beach down below. Then we're leaving the beach and the white waves at the shoreline behind as the road sweeps around a headland, taking us out over the ocean before curving back in and I can see the Atlantic surf rolling into the next sandy bay. The reason that all these T4's come here.

The pub is separated from the road by a low wall that looks like it's made of Christmas cake icing, the building itself is long, neatly painted in white, window boxes on the second floor and a charcoal-grey thatched roof. Much bigger inside than it looks from the outside, packed with visitors, holiday makers, tourists and surfers. We have to navigate our way around the bar over the course of a few trips, weaving through the crowd with our speakers, instruments and microphone stands. Large groups eating, drinking and making a lot of noise. We're going to have to make some noise too if we want to be heard, it's more of a place for ska bands.

It's after 9pm by the time we start, turning the volume up as loud as we can. A few people look over from around the bar. Hints of approval from some, an upside down smile with a raising and lowering of the head. Most British pub audiences don't usually express outward enjoyment of music in the first half of the evening regardless of what you play. The end of the evening's a totally different matter, everybody's drunk, uninhibited, senses dulled, but music can still touch the primitive parts of the brain. It can conjure up it's strange and potent magic, bring a crowd together.

When you first play gigs you have none of the songs that can guarantee this will happen. The end of the evening feels like a shipwreck, floundering on the rocks of disappointment, an audience underwhelmed. It's a heady feeling when you discover what does work, that said, it's got to be something that my stone cold sober brain doesn't feel is too cheap or cheesy.

Tonight the sea feels stormier than normal, the bar is bigger, noisier, the crowd more dispersed and distracted. There's no sense of unity, I think we might hit the rocks. At last orders a group of drunk surfers come in, all straw blonde hair, grins and sunburnt faces and they dig the music, dancing at the side of the bar as they're buying drinks. We play to them and they make so much appreciative noise that it sounds like the whole bar has come together as one, the landlord's happy and we count ourselves lucky to finish the evening on a high.

"Cheers, goodnight, thanks a lot."

The surfer guys keep forgetting they've said goodnight already, every time we take some gear out to the van they say it again. We say we're not going yet, we'll be back in a minute to get more stuff, but the next time they see us,

"Cheers, goodnight, thanks a lot."

Leaning on each other, grinning, the lager swilling around the insides of their unsteady pint glasses. Music might have touched them, but saying goodbye doesn't register. When it's our last trip we get ready to see them, to say a proper goodbye, but they've gone.

The landlord gives us a big pub breakfast the next morning, big enough to fuel anyone spending their day surfing the Atlantic. Then we're waving to all the T4's again, driving out of Croyde, back out around the headland until their numbers gradually decline as we move further away from the coast. Back to Somerset, to a little village south of Portishead, Weston-in-Gordano, sat in a low valley a mile inland from the Severn Estuary and a mile the other side to the M5 motorway.

We like to get to a gig an hour or so before we start, set up, settle in, check out the drinks arrangement. There's only one couple in the pub when we arrive, we strike up a conversation, get to know our audience even if there's only two of them. They're not planning on staying though and hadn't realised there'd be music on. He says he's a sound engineer, they're just in for a quick drink,

"I'll help you soundcheck if you want?"

Okay, why not.

He knows a lot about sound equipment, about model numbers, the x's and z's that sex up the name of fancy music gear. He runs his eyes over our stuff looking a little disappointed, raises his eyebrows at our set up. Two different speakers, everybody uses two of the same. I explain that one's battery operated for busking, he's not convinced.

He stands out front while we play a song, his head going from side to side, speaker to speaker. Jayne looks at me with an almost imperceptible shake of her head, she's mouthing a word, a name, Kenji. Kenji, the soundman at a wedding we once played, his name now synonymous with the possibility of a quirky soundcheck. Kenji had his sound desk in the next room. He'd run in through the side door, stand in the middle of the floor in front of us, knees bent, arms bent with his hands up, a kind of martial arts stance, jerking his head from left to right to left. Listening to each of the speakers but looking more like he was limbering up for a fight, one he expected to lose. Then he would rush out of the room to make some changes before returning a minute later, the same posture, the same behaviour, again and again until he was happy with the sound. I say happy but he never looked happy, just variations of anxious. Sound changes during a gig too, as a room fills with people you need to make adjustments. So Kenji would periodically appear in the middle of the dance floor, alongside the wedding guests having a boogie, his erratic behaviour out of synch with their smoother moves. Them dancing, him in his karate position, checking on how it was going, our ninja soundman fine tuning the music from next door.

Tonight is nothing like that,

"Sounds good, but you should get two of the same speakers."

Now they've heard us play they decide to stay for the first half.

A crowd of locals come along too, all standing in one big huddle together, bantering and taking the mickey out of each other. Two of them come up and chat in the break, a young couple that live close by in the village, Paul and Aileen. Paul says he plays harmonica, we suggest he goes home and gets his harps while we think of some numbers he can join us on.

The crowd get more drunk in the second half, cheering when Paul plays harmonica, he's good and it encourages more banter. As the locals leave they promise to pester the landlord for a repeat booking.

"Were there enough people for them to book us again?"

It's midnight, I'm passing Jayne the mic stands in the pub car park, so dark outside she's having to feel for them, the metal is cold and damp in the night air,

"The locals seemed to think so."

I can hear her sliding the mic stands under the bed, hear them clunking in next to each other, at least we've decided on a place to store them.

Then we're feeling around for our wash kits, we made a pact to brush our teeth every night, too easy just to roll into bed at the end of an evening and not bother. Standing outside, at the back of the pub, my eyes have adjusted a little more to the pitch black. Can we really make this all work, I can't tell. We climb in, slamming the side door shut, we don't even need to put the curtains up.

3. ONE MORE CUP OF COFFEE

Where am I? Jayne's nudging me, letting me know it's time for a cup of coffee. She's not usually the first to open her eyes, but where am I? I'm waking up in the same bed but always in a different place. It'll come to me, I know I'll figure it out in a minute. Daylight's streaming in through the windows, I remember, we're in the pub car park at the back of The White Hart in Weston-in-Gordano.

I open the side door and sit on the edge of the bed, it's warm outside, the sun's shining, making it's way up into a bright blue sky. Over the hedge are green fields leading to low lying hills in the distance. Balancing the camping stove on a box lid I boil some water, open the sunroof so the steam can curl it's way up and out. I gently pour the first of the boiled water into the filter, soaking the fresh coffee until it starts to drip through, moving the filter back and forth across the cups, more steam curling up and out of the roof.

Jayne's propped her pillows up on the side of

the bed, I do the same so we can look out over the hedge and the green fields. This is what we did this for, the feeling of being out there, nomads I suppose, living in the spaces in between.

I guess we've always been looking to be out there, always been looking for something, ever since we met there's been a restlessness tugging away, both of us wondering whether to listen to that wandering voice. Ever since we met at university in Hull over twenty years ago, Jayne studying Italian, yearning for a change of scenery. I was doing Maths, mine was nothing to do with aptitude, just a means of carrying on being a student. After that, life followed it's irregular, convoluted paths, like the steam rising up from the coffee cups, swirling in unforeseen directions. Me getting into juggling whilst training to be a teacher and before we knew it we were travelling with a circus, then another one the next year. Strange corners and bends, running away from the circus. Running away from a circus is more common than you think, it even has a name, a verb, *to scarper*. So we scarpered to a bedsit in Brighton, to odd jobs before Jayne worked for VIVA! The Vegetarian's International Voice for Animals, I became an Alexander Technique teacher whilst working as a telephone debt collector. Then feeling the pressure to get on the property ladder and the nearest town with affordable property was Hastings so we bought a small flat there. I worked as a bank cashier, Jayne got a sales job and we settled into an everyday nine to five life.

The thing was, we never really settled, definitely not when we got into the local music scene, spectators at first, no thoughts of participating or performing. In all our time together music had been ebbing and flowing like the tide, sometimes close, sometimes further away but always there, we were always playing. Singing songs in the kitchen or round campfires on holidays, scraps of lyrics and ideas, home recordings we were too shy to share with anyone else. When we started to play gigs the tide came in, flooding right over and around us, we couldn't ignore it, we had to go with it to see where it would take us. We had to cut the ropes, set sail and leave our home behind, see if a pocketful of songs would keep us afloat.

I'm hanging on to the last few mouthfuls of coffee, lukewarm in the bottom of the cup, maybe I'll make another one. Far away the hills suspend a small section of motorway, traffic quietly going up and down. I didn't notice it at first, caught up in my thoughts and the green fields and the sunny day. We'll be on that motorway soon, trucking to the next destination. Holding back from packing the stove up means we can stay a little longer, I know when I go to put it away, it'll be our signal to move on.

We used to get fresh coffee beans from a local health food store, grind them ourselves. Once when we were buying a big paper bag of beans we asked the guy at the till if he'd tried them? No, he said,

"I don't borrow energy from the future."

We might need to borrow some today, two gigs, the first in a cafe in a park in Swindon.

The cafe, when we get there, is a serving hatch on the side of an old brick building. Various paths around the park come together at a courtyard with tables and chairs, the coffee counter on one side and a large pond on the other. We set up with the pond behind us facing mostly empty seating. A mum is sitting with a young child in a buggy, facing away from us, one hand gently rolling the wheels back and forth while the other holds her phone. An elderly gentleman is reading the Sunday newspapers. We can see the smiling face of Matthew behind the counter as he serves up takeaway drinks to passers by. When we start to play the mum stays where she is but turns the child's buggy round so it can see us, the old man carries on reading the paper.

After a while a couple of homeless guys come along, walking across the grass, bypassing the pathways. They don't use the cafe chairs but sit on a small wall nearby. Each one has a crumpled plastic carrier bag, their faces and hands tanned from the sun, sharing a can of something, sharing a roll-up too, taking turns, one smokes while the other drinks. Sunlight shines down on them, they lean back and close their eyes, soaking it up,

"All day long," they call out to us after every song,

"All day long."

Matthew's a positive guy, we make light of the small number of people there and say yes to another cup of coffee,

"Where do you guys live again?"

It's a question I know we're going to have to get used to answering,

"There."

I point over to the van we've been allowed to bring inside the park to load our gear,

"Okay," says Matthew but my answer hangs in the air, both too simple and too complicated at the same time. Jayne and I stumble over an explanation, blowing the hot liquid in our cups to cool them down, smiling at him and each other, trying to give the impression that everything's fine, it's our choice, we know what we're doing.

"Oh, right," says Matthew.

We could try a different answer next time.

In Tetbury there's a restaurant that advertises pizza and live music on Sunday nights. Young good looking waiting staff in clean white shirts and black aprons hurry across a wood panelled floor, twisting and turning around pine tables. Well spoken and friendly, one of them comes along while we're setting up to ask us when we'd like our food. When she sees our indecision she says she'll be back in a minute and glides off. If we eat before we play it means we'll feel totally full and not like playing at all. If we have it in the 15 minute break in the middle then they'll have to bring it out at just the right time and we'll be in a rush to eat it. If we have it at the end the kitchen will probably be closed or at the back end of it's shift and the staff will want to tidy and clean up around us.

As far as I can tell nobody eating here has come along for the music. Sitting in tight groups of twos and fours, on high-backed heavy chairs, their subdued voices murmur up into the vaulted roof. I go to the gents, on the wall in the toilets is a listing of what's on on Sunday nights.

An American businessman comes over in the break, he sounds like he's from Texas, we ask him what brings him all the way over to the Cotswolds? Something to do with oil but he brushes that aside, moves the conversation on, he wants to talk guitars, wants to talk about his collection back home, wishes he could bring one of them with him on his business trips.

We have our pizza at the end and eat half of it as the staff clear up, skating around us. They box the rest and we eat it in the van in the deep shadows of some off road parking down the other end of Tetbury high street. High fences and bushes on the other side of the road screen us from a row of stone houses, screen us from any watchful eyes. No one sees us as we slip out of our front doors and climb into the back to sleep.

We need a shower and look for a campsite that might have decent facilities. There's one not far away with rave reviews about it's modernised heated shower blocks but the downside when we get there is the lengthy check-in. At reception they scrutinize new arrivals with a lengthy form to fill in: address, email, phone number, length of stay, a photocopy of identification. So much information to sleep in a field.

No chance of choosing our own space either, we're not allowed. Another member of staff walks briskly in front of us in his green fleece uniform to show us exactly where to park. Driving slowly past manicured lawns, little fences and pristine white signs before he points at our space. Indicating with arm gestures precisely which one it is, no room for interpretation,

"Enjoy your stay," he says with a smile that soon fades.

We're regretting our choice but change our mind when we get to the newly built shower block. Underfloor heating, clean spacious cubicles, top of the range shower heads pumping out seriously hot water. Jayne and I stand under them for ages, emerging red faced, the steam radiating off us in the cool of the early evening.

I cook supper with the camping stove set up on a chair, crouching down, balancing the pans. The man in the caravan next door comes out and asks if we'd like his old fold-up table, they no longer need it. He's been watching me make the meal, thought we might find it useful. I thank him for his kindness and we make small talk about camping. He and his wife have been coming for years and started their camping days with a tent. Now they come in a large caravan, all mod-cons, all their household appliances, everything they need.

He looks over at his caravan, through the window his wife is watching television, the bright blue screen illuminating the inside,

"It's not as much fun as it was back then."

He says goodnight, makes his way in, the caravan door closing with a little click. We put our new table up, finish supper and go and take another shower.

Arranging gigs a long way from home is luck of the draw, we've no idea what they'll be like when we get there. Mostly it's been about whether they want to put a date in the diary and agree to some kind of payment.

This is the kind of logic that's led us, over the course of a few days, to make our way to Ramsgate on the east coast of Kent. A cafe bar that has space in the back where they sometimes have live music. The landlady has agreed to pay us a decent fee, maybe more depending on how many people come along.

We get there early evening and she and her husband and their dog are sat round a table in the small empty cafe.

"Would you like something to eat?"

Her accent is transatlantic, American sounding. Long wavy black hair, olive skin, dressed in a silk gown, her sandals make a shuffling sound on the floor as she shows us the small counter where there's some food in serving trays. We take a little look, peering in cautiously,

"No thanks, we've already eaten but thanks anyway."

"You guys go ahead and set up in the back room."

We go into the back room. Clothes on rails, a sofa, a mannequin, a selection of school chairs and little round tables. A screen separates off another section, darker, messier, it looks like there's a bed and kitchen in there, it's hard to tell.

"How many people usually come along to the gigs here?"

"You never know how it's going to go."

She's moving a few things around and wandering in and out of the room as we finish setting up.

We all sit together for a drink at a table in the cafe, she says business has been difficult recently, slow, not much passing trade. The front door opens, we all turn to see who it is, it's a friend of theirs coming in for a pint. He goes and sits on his own. There's a suggestion we might want to start playing, maybe people will come in. We go through to the back room again, the three of them and the dog follow behind us.

In between songs we try to have conversations with our little audience, the atmosphere reminds me of a breakfast room at a B&B, the only thing absent is the sound of cutlery against plates or bread popping up in a toaster. The dog is a useful distraction, deflecting attention away from human embarrassment. He thought he was in for a normal quiet night and isn't used to all the fuss being made of him. After half an hour we suggest perhaps we play 15 minutes more then call it a night.

"Good idea."

As we're packing up, with more efficiency than usual, the landlady comes over, sandals clopping along the floor, big doleful eyes, holding a cheque book limply. She looks worried,

"How much did we agree on?"

It's not in us to take her money, we tell her to forget about it.

A year or so later, friends of ours from Ramsgate talked about having been to the same place. They said we should have taken the money, they also said they once had some food there, something like hot cross buns and gravy.

Loading up the van we talk about how soon we might be able to forget the experience, about where we might park up for the night. Choosing where to sleep has become a daily challenge. Easy enough if the gig has a car park but if it doesn't or we don't have a booking then we have to decide where we'll feel safe, where we'll go unnoticed. Sometimes it's hard to find a place we're happy with. Last night we pulled into a space, a quiet backstreet, tired and ready to sleep. Just as Jayne turned off the ignition, a curtain was drawn open in the upstairs of a nearby house, we could see a silhouette of a man standing in the window, his hands on his hips as he looked out. He stayed there, not moving, what was he doing, was he looking at us? We couldn't tell, after five minutes it didn't feel right and we had to move on, settle for second best, a lay-by out of town.

We've booked a few gigs around our old stomping ground in East Sussex, it was hard not to. Up the road from where we used to live we sometimes modelled for an art class run by a painter and jazz musician. Ben's asked us to come for another sitting.

Tucked away in a big detached house on the west hill in Hastings, hidden by trees, down the end of a long driveway that leads from one of the narrow roads up on the high part of town. The Beacon, a home to artists and their studios. Ben's in his 70's, calm and kind in soft corduroy trousers and knitted jumpers, his movements are slow and gentle. We're in a large room on the ground floor, near double doors that lead out to an overgrown, green and sloping garden. Modelling fully clothed, costume life drawing it's called, artists with their easels in a circle around us while we play songs and tunes. Relaxed and informal, we don't even have to keep still or anything, just sit and make music. We play while the artists sweep their arms around canvasses and sketch pads, each one at a different pace, focussing, then pausing, tilting their head and looking some more before carrying on again. Looking at us but not looking at us.

Little conversations bubble up softly in the silence between the music. Soothing and peaceful, the atmosphere's very intimate, the artists are very appreciative. There's an interval in the middle for coffee. The group stand around the easels and empty chairs in the break, admiring each other's work, critical of their own and complementary about everyone else's. We open up about our situation, our new lifestyle on the road, ask if anyone has ideas of where we could go in the winter, we've no plans other than being warm and self sufficient. One of them says they have friends that go down to the south of Spain every winter, somewhere near Cadiz, it's warm enough to camp. We make a mental note.

At the end we sometimes get given some of the artwork. It's one of the nicest gigs we play. When we exchange gentle hugs with Ben at the end, there's a sparkle in his eye as he thanks us and pays us, it feels like it should be the other way round.

We ring Martini Bob, ask him if he wants to meet up for coffee,

"I'm at work."

Easy to forget people keep regular hours. He suggests we meet later on at The Sovereign Light Cafe, the one in Bexhill, the one in the Keane song.

"So how's it all going?" he says when we get there. I'm not sure how to answer,

"Alright, early days, still things to get rid of."

Bob says he'll take our spare speaker, stick it in his garage for the time being. He's getting rid of extra weight too, he's got a new fitness regime, he's had a health scare, is keeping himself busy exercising, has another trip to Las Vegas booked next month. We say we'll stay in touch.

In East Sussex there's a pub near the tiny village of Chailey, another one in our old stomping ground, set back on a lazy curve of a country road. It's a big place, rambling inside, lots of corners and cosy nooks. The owner Robin is a real gent, very polite with a relaxed charm, suntanned, dressed in slacks and pastel sportsman's sweaters. He even asks if we need help carrying our gear in, always complements us on our retro cases, quick to offer us a drink. The feeling of being welcome counts for even more now we haven't got a home.

A young guy in a bomber jacket comes in as we're setting up, dyed black hair and Doc Marten boots, carrying a clipboard. He's with his girlfriend and they sit on a sofa where they can see us. Before we start he comes up to say hello, he works freelance for PRS, the Performing Rights Society, says he's here to make a note of the songs we play. He likes live music, comes out to gigs whenever he can. His girlfriend comes along too but she usually gets bored and leaves halfway through. After a gig he sends the list of songs played back to PRS. PRS pay royalties for every public performance of a song at licensed venues.

We include plenty of original material in the set, announcing the titles before and after every song so he can make a note on his clipboard. In the break we clarify anything he might have missed.

In the second half someone says there's a birthday in the house so we lead everyone in a chorus of 'Happy Birthday'. A boozy late night version, the room full of drunken strangers singing good wishes. The PRS guy announces he has to write this on his list too, his girlfriend decided to stay, maybe it's the mood in the bar, cheerful, easy going and friendly.

At the end of the night Robin says he's looking to sell up soon, retire to the seaside and leave the challenge of running a big pub to someone else, he's not sure if the next owner will carry on with the music.

We're skirting round the edge of our old stomping ground, retreading old paths, revisiting old haunts. Like a gastropub in Plumpton, on a leafy winding B road, a yellow half moon on a blue sign high up near it's roof. Jimmy Page's local when he lived in the area. There's a large oil painting on the wall inside, it shows the bar crammed full of all the locals at the time, and Jimmy's in it. I doubt he's played one of these gigs though. The bar is small, L-shaped, and we're in the short section of it so we can't see anyone. Most people are dining just around the corner, we can only hear them if they clap at the end of a song. Tonight though, a couple of young women are down from London with their dog, a toffee coloured spaniel called Treacle, they're sat in the small space in front of us. Treacle's sensitive to noise so we agree to call a halt to any clapping and go for a thumbs up instead. It makes for an even quieter gig but Treacle likes it and the ladies give us regular thumbs up, sometimes two.

The gig doesn't pay much but the manager

and chef's a lovely guy, Richard, always a wide grin on his face and beads of sweat on his brow. Makes a point of coming for a chat at the end of the night even though he's tired after a long day in his tiny kitchen. He says he's looking at moving pubs, thinking of going for another chef's job in Brighton, isn't sure how long they'll keep the music on here. Sometimes gigs feel like they're falling like dominoes.

A big question when selling our flat was what postal address to use once we were on the road. We needed one for all the usual tax and insurance reasons but who could we ask to take it in? It's not a question you can ask anybody, regardless of how good a friend they are, it's got to feel right, like you know it won't bother them however long it's for.

Around the time we put our flat on the market we met a couple at a gig. They were on holiday, by chance they'd spotted one of our posters on the window outside a pub we were playing. At first they were the only two people in the bar so we got talking. Shinina's small but carries herself very upright, hair down to her waist, a large wrap around shawl draped around her shoulders. Carlos is quieter, more reserved, into motorbikes and vans. Shinina's the kind of person who's quick to get to the deeper questions in life, a spiritual person, looking for meaning, looking into our eyes to see what lies behind.

At the end of that night, as we were unplugging equipment, coiling up cables, clearing away, Jayne said to me,

"Did you mention to Shinina about us selling our flat?"

I said no I hadn't said anything. Our flat was fresh on the market back then, our decision was still too fragile to share.

"Well she just said that while she was watching us she kept getting the message *'no mortgage'*."

So that was our second endorsement. Along with Martini Bob's roll of the dice approval we had Shinina's spiritual premonition, both telling us to go for it.

We went to stay with Shinina and Carlos for a weekend. From that point on they were intimately bound up with our journey and the right people to ask about taking in our post. They were cool about it, said yes straight away.

So we go to collect our mail, the initial stack of envelopes from changing addresses before it hopefully dwindles to next to nothing. They live in one of the small towns a few miles outside Maidstone, the heart of the commuter belt, full of schools and cul-de-sacs and little recreation areas. Only an hour from London, every street leads to a maze of others, two cars in each driveway. Their home's at the end of a row of red-brick terraced houses down a dead-end lane. Carlos takes a walk around the outside of our van when we get there, making the right kind of noises as he circles around it, looking it over. He's a petrol head, a handy guy too and helps remove the swivel attachment on the passenger seat to lower it down by a couple of inches. I jump in, tilt the seat back to it's upright position, stretch, rock my body back and forth, feeling the relief as my head's now completely clear of the roof.

Then we drive up to Lincoln, a couple of nights pitched up by a lake in a campsite out of town. By the time we checkout the tranquillity has rubbed off on us, we're fresh again, ready for the weekend. We've no idea about our two gigs in Lincoln, both booked on the phone. The first one, Saturday night at the top end of town.

When we pull into the car park, there's a side door propped open, I can hear it's busy before we even step inside. A huge pub, at the bar a member of staff points through the throng of people to a table of four, laden with empty glasses. The landlord, drinking with his wife and friends.

We make our way over and stand beside them, they're laughing, a smell of aftershave and perfume heavy in the air. They stop laughing and turn and look us up and down, obvious who the landlord is, the largest of the four of them. A chunky gold chain around his neck and gold rings on his fingers, he gives us a beefy handshake, everyone else goes back to their drink. We ask where he wants us to play, he points up some nearby stairs. To avoid having to come and ask him later we check if we can stay the night in the car park. He doesn't reply straight away, instead he looks at his wife, after a few moments he says,

"Yeah, that's okay."

There are raised seating areas, each one up four or five steps, one of them has been roped off for us. Our platform to blast out the Saturday night entertainment.

"Sorry about this," Jayne feels responsible for booking the gig, she's giving herself a hard time as we're setting up the mic stands, plugging the gear in. The place is boozy, noisy, no one's smiling at us, some people are trying to make eye contact for the wrong reason, the tranquillity of camping by the lake has long gone.

We start, turn the volume up, keep the tempo up, play anything that might have popular appeal to get us through the first set and go the distance. At half-time I put my guitar back in it's stand, relieved we've made it this far. I think we've done okay, some of the crowd have nodded into their pint glasses, some have tapped their feet, no one's thrown anything, we've survived. Then the landlord comes up the stairs red faced, bullish,

"Here's your money, pack your things, the gig's over."

His big fist has a roll of bank notes in it, he pushes them into my hand,

"I'm putting the jukebox on."

He says people will leave if he doesn't, then turns, goes back down the steps. Jayne and I look at each other,

"What?"

I can't see anyone leaving, there's more people here than when we started. This has never happened before. Embarrassed, nervous, confused, shaking a bit as we start putting the gear away. The jukebox kicks in, pumping out dance music. People around the bar are looking over, watching us packing up, even they don't know what's going on. Let's get this done quickly and get out of here, we chuck everything in their cases, not bothering about packing things in any order.

Then we realise something, we've been paid, we've got the money, we're leaving, we're free to go. The feeling of dejection turns to relief, puts a spring in our step, we carry as much gear as we can through the crowd and out to the van. Jayne gets in the driver seat, starts the engine while I go back in for the last few bits. As I'm heading to the open door, the landlord stops me,

"You can still stay the night in the car park."

Jayne laughs when I tell her, pulling out of our space and onto the road,

"He said what?"

We drive out to the campsite by the lake to see if our space by the water's still available.

Next morning, despite laughing it off, we're still trying to forget the experience, put it behind us, but we can't undo it. Maybe Lincoln isn't for us, maybe we've chosen the wrong town to come and play gigs in. There's another one still to play this afternoon, what'll that be like? Better remind ourselves what we're in for, take a look at their website. It's at The Strugglers Inn, says it's named after the place where people used to watch public hangings by the castle walls, the struggling bodies of those condemned to death, an audience gathered to witness them writhing in agony as they hung from the noose. Maybe we should leave town early?

Then we're there, pulling up outside, the pub standing alone at the corner of the castle walls, close enough that you could roll down the embankments and bump into it's side wall. The Strugglers is run by Anna, she's friendly when we walk in, excited to have an act from out of town play at her pub. It's small inside, very busy, a separate little snug to the right of the front door as you go in. To the left the bar runs lengthways, only just room for the tables, we have to turn sideways to carry our gear through. There are people sat in the space at the end where we're going to play, Anna wastes no time in telling them they have to move to make room for the music. With the authority of a headmistress the customers are quick to oblige, immediately picking up their glasses and relocating to another table.

Sunday afternoons run like clockwork, Anna says to take a break at 6pm because that's when the raffle is. She calls out the numbers for the prizes then brings out a big tray of salty chips and bread rolls for everyone.

I load a chip butty up with ketchup and get chatting to a guy, Mike, who offers me a drink. Mike's wearing a faded green baseball cap low down over his eyes, a neatly trimmed beard.

He's complementary about our music and plays the guitar himself. Him and his wife are thinking of starting a duo to play around the pubs in Lincoln. I tell him about our experience last night, maybe when they start gigging they should avoid that one. He knows the place, can't believe we played there, shakes his head,

"They don't know good music when they hear it."

Jayne meets a woman drinking at the bar, she runs a pub the other side of town, says to give her a call about a gig the next time we're in the area. Maybe Lincoln is for us after all. Kicking off the second half, I look out, there's a cheer of appreciation from a roomful of friendly faces, it feels like we're back somewhere we belong. Anna says to get in touch when we're next up this way, we know we'll be back at The Strugglers before too long.

We had no idea what to expect from that weekend and neither of us have any idea what to expect at the next gig either, a truck stop. Jayne's spoken to the owner Karl a few times on the phone to arrange it, he loves his music, likes to talk too, he and Jayne have had some long conversations but she's none the wiser as to what it'll actually be like.

Suffolk, eastbound on the A14, we pull off the dual carriageway when we see a big old beige sign high up on a rusty pole, The Orwell Crossing Truck

Stop, something else written on the sign has been scrubbed out. We park up beside the lorries, rows of freight probably heading for the port of Felixstowe eight miles down the road.

Inside, the service area is divided down the middle. To the left is the cafeteria with sandy coloured floor tiles, vinyl tablecloths, a couple of lorry drivers at separate tables tucking into big plates of food. Along the length of the wall there's a thin shelf that's high up and out of reach, small collections of pottery vases, jugs and jars.

On the other side, to the right as you go in, is an open area with a stage, a dance floor, an old armchair and a sofa, chairs stacked up around the edge of a maroon carpet. Different patterns have come and gone over the years, each one has left something behind.

Karl's behind the counter at reception, well over six foot, big frame, black beard, wavy hair swept back and down to his shoulders. Quiet and reserved, awkward at first, the conversation doesn't get going until we start talking about music. He becomes animated, he loves karaoke, wants to show us his karaoke machine, they put on special nights at the weekend. The area for the music is pretty big, Karl's proud of his stage set up, the lighting rig, the black backdrop, the equipment. A few chairs and a couple of tables are set out for the audience.

At the start of the gig this consists of Karl, Mike the night security guy, a lorry driver who's wandered over from the cafeteria to sit at the edge by the far wall and two middle-aged couples. The two couples have driven out specially to see the music, they're dressed up for a night out and have different expectations of what they've come for. One of them asks me to play 'Cavatina' on the guitar, the haunting, sad and emotional classical guitar piece from the film *The Deer Hunter*. The other couple want something they can dance to, preferably a jive. We disappoint both of them, they sit and sip their drinks, at the end of each song there's the sound of a few hands clapping in a large room.

Just before the break a guy comes in and sits in the old armchair, sinking down low in between it's high sides. At half time he comes up and introduces himself, he's American, short with the build and close cropped hair of someone in the military, a ribbed sweater, khaki trousers and Timberland boots. He's not a trucker but he likes to drive out to the lorry park now and again for the music, says he sometimes acts as an agent for bands and musicians in the area. He strongly advises we develop a Cajun sound, there's an intensity in his face and eyes when he's talking. I say we like Cajun music and will give it some thought, he's insistent and serious about it, says to get in touch if we do.

The second half of the evening is similar to the first. People in an audience think you can't hear what they're saying when you're on stage but you'd be surprised how much talk travels. I can hear the couple that want to jive voicing their displeasure to each other. At one point the wife leans over to her husband, gesturing with her head towards us, she says,

"Do you think these two are a couple?"

I come straight back over the mic,

"Yes we are."

She looks embarrassed, I wish I'd kept my mouth shut. I notice the trucker's gone, I don't remember seeing him leave.

At the end Mike the security guy buys two of our CDs, Jayne and I claw some self-esteem back from his expression of kindness. Mike's head and body are rectangular, he's dangerous-looking on the outside but he's all soft and sentimental on the inside. Karl seems happy too, maybe just having music here is enough, he says to come back again later in the year for another gig, a repeat booking. We say that would be great, Mike says he'll be pleased to see us. Carrying our gear out past the reception, we can see our van on the CCTV monitors under Mike's watchful eye. The American guy calls out a goodnight, reminding us again about a Cajun sound.

The next morning we go in to use the showers, the place is much busier, the cafe full of lorry drivers eating big cooked breakfasts, drinking steaming mugs of tea. Mike is just finishing his shift, Karl will be in soon to start his. Over by the dance floor the American guy is asleep in the high sided armchair.

Whitstable's a small seaside town on the north coast of Kent. Famous for it's oysters, it also has a lot of live music at weekends. On Sundays the bars stagger the start times of their bands, arrange them through the afternoon so locals can do the rounds and pretty much see them all. A music pub crawl from midday onwards. The last main watering hole is a venue right on the beach, the end of the line for most drinkers, the bands at this place finish at 8pm, the pub even closes soon after.

There's one more gig in town though, one that starts at 8pm. At the end of a long boozy Sunday in Whitstable, on a small back street that runs parallel to the high street. We've got ourselves a gig at this one, a pub called The Smack.

Driving through town early evening I can see the effects of a long day of drinking, people meandering off pavements onto the road, back onto the pavement again, making their irregular way home. We park briefly outside The Smack to unload, put the van in a nearby car park and walk back, it's empty apart from the barmaid. The pub is small, the bar is a concentric square in the middle it so they can serve drinks on three of it's sides. At the furthest corner from the entrance is a small raised stage, about a foot off the ground and just big enough for us both to stand on without falling off. Plenty of time to set up, no distractions, just us and the barmaid, she even gives us a drink. It's cosy in here, if only there were a few people,

"Oh, you'll get a few drift in during the

evening."

She's right. They come in gradually, ones, twos and small groups. The Sunday diehards, musos checking out the live music, people who can handle a long day of drinking, the ones that can keep going, people with no one to go home to. Most seem to know each other, talking between themselves while we play, quieter than most pubs, more respectful, more aware of the musicians, taking the time to give applause at the end of each song.

A guy comes up to us in the break. Unassuming, white hair that's thinning on top, wire frame spectacles, says he likes what we're doing. Says he nearly didn't come tonight but glad he did, then he goes back to his seat.

"You've got the seal of approval if Jim likes your music."

Another older guy is standing beside us with a pint glass in his hand, there's kindness in his face, a twinkle in his eye, he has a salt and pepper goatee beard, more salt than pepper. Introduces himself as Bob, says the guy that just came up to us is Jim Leverton, bass player with Caravan,

"He's played with everybody."

Bob's a big music lover, has done the rounds this afternoon, sober as far as I can tell, impressive given the amount of bands he's seen today.

"Can I get you both a drink?"

He pulls a handful of change out of his trouser pocket, signals to the barmaid to get us whatever we want and puts the coins on the bar.

We play our second set, more drifters come in. The atmosphere is warm, fuzzy, nobody wants to be anywhere else, there's nowhere else to go. At the end of the night Bob says he'll look out for when we're next playing in Whitstable, offers us both another drink. We say yes, agree to stay for one more, he puts his pint glass on the bar and his hand goes into his pocket again, his big pocketful of change. He places more coins on the counter, it's last orders but nobody in here shows any sign of leaving. They're hanging on to Sunday night, hanging on to the final hour of the weekend, we take our drinks to a free table and join them.

Jayne's had a couple of glasses by the time we leave. Too much to drive, we decide to sleep in the car park, the one down the road, where we're parked already. The orange light from a couple of street lamps illuminate parts of it, the rest is in darkness. Bordered by garden fences, small bushes and trees growing out of backyards, no lights on in any of the houses, quiet. The side door of the van is heavy, always shuts with a loud slam, we make sure we only have to do it once then try to synchronise it quickly with the central locking. A single flash of all four indicator lights when the doors lock, then quiet again. A few cars are here, it'll fill up in the morning though, it's just a stones throw from the high street. Charges kick in at 8am, that'll be when the cars arrive, we need to be gone by then, we set the alarm to leave before anyone might see us. Best not draw attention to ourselves so we can come again.

Next morning, early, we're tired after the late night and drive two minutes up the road to Tankerton. An esplanade, a mile long strip of lawn, park benches every ten or fifteen metres. A slope of wild grass leads down to a shingle beach, the little triangular tops of the roofs of the beach huts just visible from the road. Monday morning, windy, every bench on the grass is deserted. We sit in the back of the van, on the side, brew coffee and look out to sea, the sound of the wind rocking us back and forth, my eyes wanting to close and sleep some more.

Sometimes being on the road, moving all the time, is tiring. More tiring than when we had a home, when we had a place of our own to go to. A home, a sanctuary, a hideaway to recover in, a front door to close behind us, to get ready for life again. Simple things like taking a shower, doing our laundry, staying in one place for a day or two, all these are a refuge at times.

With a couple of free days, maybe we'll stay on the coast, not drive far. We look for a campsite and one comes up nearby on the Isle of Sheppey, we can see the island from where we're parked up now. Far over to our left, the Thames Estuary, our panoramic view that stretches across a wide expanse of water to the North Sea on our right.

The campsite only has five pitches, I better ring and check they have space. A guy answers, a strong cockney accent, no doubt where he's from,

"Sorry mate, we're full, what sort of van 'av

you got?"

I explain it's a VW T4 sort of thing, small really.

"That's alright, we'll getcha parked up on the side."

Says his name's Steve, and that one of the campers is leaving tomorrow, we can park on the drive and move into their space when they've gone.

We drive over the bridge, the Sheppey Crossing flyover that lifts you up and over the Swale and onto the island. Then a left to Queenborough, through a housing estate, each road getting smaller, narrower until they run out and we're on a dirt track leading to the site.

I say a site but it isn't a site as such, it's a house, a bungalow, the campsite is it's front garden and driveway. Room for five motor homes, each little pitch separated by a low hedge, colourful shrubs, flowers and bushes in pots, each one has its own picnic table too. There's a covered seating area by the house, a toilet and shower block, an immaculate front lawn with a small pagoda, a rockery with more colourful plants. Paradise for a garden gnome but I can't see any.

Steve comes to greet us, affable, easy to talk to, says we can have a fire in the evening if we want, we can use the brazier in the seating area. Jayne'll always light a fire if she's given the chance, she had an astrology reading once, her whole chart centred in the fire signs, her love of it is written in the stars.

A fire's a reminder of home too, we go to

source some logs and take a walk with an empty rucksack to the nearby town of Queenborough. Back down the dirt road, back through the terraced houses then round a large overgrown wasteland destined for some future development. Past factories, small businesses, yards full of lorries until we're back among the terraced houses of a town again. The road into Queenborough runs along Queenborough Creek, low tide and the boats along both sides are resting on the mud.

There's a pub in the small town that has live music at weekends, we go in and ask about a gig. They're booked up far ahead, the landlady says she wants to see us play live somewhere first. We let her know of a couple of gigs in the next few months that aren't too far away but I'm not sure she'll remember.

In the evening, as twilight turns to night, with the wood burning in the fire pit, industrial lights come on far over on the horizon. You can see them in the distance out over the dark water of the Swale and the River Medway. A couple from one of the camper vans see that we're having a fire and ask if they can join us, they're from Whitstable, how about that,

"We just played a gig there last night."

Mike and Jeanette, Jeanette's face is soft and kind, Mike's is round and friendly, a big bushy moustache that droops round the edges of his mouth, he asks,

"Where are you guys from?"

"Good question."

We sit round the fire and forego the simple answer, explain our circumstances, our lifestyle choice. We talk about Whitstable, about music, they love live music and go out to see bands in town a lot. They say to let them know when we're next playing and we can park up and sleep on their driveway.

On the last day we sit and have coffee with Steve, he's always up for a chat. Him and his wife named the campsite Leobay in honour of their grandson, Leo, they lost him in a tragic accident when he was very young. They put their love into the place, a living memory dedicated to him, we can feel it. We thank him for his warm and welcome hospitality, feel certain we'll be back. Steve says he'll always find a space on the drive for us.

We've booked gigs all over the place. Some because they have credibility, some just because they pay, some don't pay anything at all, some are for charity. Maybe they might've sounded good, sounded like they'd be fun or could lead to something, you never know. We drive down to Dartmouth, a pub in the middle of town with a good reputation for live music, a lot of under the radar musicians that are on tour play there. The owner isn't around, he's gone sailing overnight but his mum is, she makes us welcome. It's a quiet gig, just a couple of tables with a handful of people sat at each, it's light outside until late, we're playing by the window and can see people walk by but not many come in.

Next morning we head out early, two gigs, the first one, a charity event in Somerset. Two small stages side-by-side in adjacent marquees, while one act plays the other gets ready next door. It's a hot day, most people chose to sit outside on the grass eating burgers and ice cream, a few of them stand and watch at the open side of the empty marquees. Mostly local performers, there's an entrance fee to raise funds for charity and someone goes round with a hat and collects donations after each set to cover the band's expenses. We get about £15 and spend half of it at the ice cream van.

Then on to Okehampton, a small town in Devon, just off the main road that runs across the top of Dartmoor. A once a month event in a community hall in town, £2 entry, the money covers the hall expenses. There's around twenty five people in the audience so the chairs are arranged in a semi-circle around the performers. Four acts, the quality of the music is good, the last act are a duo from Plymouth. A young good-looking couple of guys with long hair and pretty faces, a great sound and good songs, they even have record company interest. They've come a distance tonight and I guess so have we, so the organisers, Phil and Anna, split the money between us and we get £15 to add to the same amount we got earlier in the day. Phil and Anna say they have a dream to hit the road with their music too some day.

4. A THOUSAND MILES

Whenever we can we take the chance to get clean, have a shower. We look for a leisure centre, I call ahead. It saves the embarrassment of asking them to their face if they say no to the question,

"Do you have a price for using a shower and change facility?"

Instead, I try to speak clearly on the phone, to sound confident and respectable. Calling it a 'shower and change facility' makes it all above board, normal. 'Price' clearly states our intention to pay for the privilege too. The answer can be a straightforward 'no', or it can be,

"No, but you can pay for a swim."

Not ideal, an expensive way to have a shower. We're not bothered about having a swim, paying £10 for the two of us to get clean doesn't seem worth it. Sometimes the person answering the phone doesn't know the answer, has to go away and check, sometimes they know straight away, replying with the perfect answer,

"Yes, it costs 80p."

Mostly it's around £2, we choose a time to go in when there's hardly anyone around, the changing room's mostly empty. You get used to leaning against the push button showers that cut out if you don't keep them pressed in, Jayne says she has a technique for double pressing them so they last longer.

There's no time to find a shower at the moment though, we're going straight from Okehampton to Dover, catching the late-night ferry to France, we'll pull over to sleep as soon as we get there. Our next destination is Austria.

As an unknown act getting booked to play a music festival is a lottery. A lottery with very little chance of success, even less of being paid. Friends and people we meet might say,

"Hey, I went to this great festival, you should play there."

But music festivals get hundreds, if not thousands of applications to play (if they even have applications at all). They have no reason or need to book or pay acts that nobody has heard of, these acts won't sell festival tickets. We have a friend who got booked by an agent to play Glastonbury Festival and he spent his time there transporting his gear in a wheelbarrow between various small stages, playing numerous gigs, all unpaid. He retains a bitter memory of the experience.

However, there's one type of music festival you can apply for with a higher chance of getting in plus you'll earn money when you're there and get travel expenses. This is a street music or busking festival. They occur all over Europe, if you're chosen then you get to travel to a cool city, stay in a hotel, play music, meet interesting people and earn some money too.

We're on our way to Linz in Austria, a big busking event held on the streets of the city every summer, Pflasterspektakel it's called. They wrote earlier in the year to tell us we'd got in, they'll pay us generous travelling expenses, put us up in accommodation, feed us and we'll keep the money we earn busking over the two and a bit days.

The plan is to get there the day before the festival starts. Around 700 miles, every few hours we pull off the motorway, take a break from the impatient lorry drivers in the slow lane of the autobahn. It's July, the country's in summer holiday mode and everyone's on vacation.

Every service area is full of hot, sweaty families in cars bulging with luggage, more stuff on the top in roof racks. Standing round the outside of their cars in their t-shirts, shorts and flip flops, the windows and doors open, smoking, drinking from bottles and cans. When we can we grab one of the picnic tables so we can put the stove up, brew a coffee or make a meal but they're mostly taken. We try a couple of times to get a shower at the motorway services but they're either too busy or out of order and we resign ourselves to a strip wash. With the curtains up, I boil some water on the box lid and we take it in turns to get in the back and get clean. The sound of cars pulling up next to us at short intervals, excited children springing out of cars, German voices, doors slamming.

At the Austrian border, Linz is less than 100 miles away. We buy a vignette, pay the toll for using the motorways but decide to come off the big roads. A smaller road follows the Danube, follows the contours of the hills, past grand houses, dotted here and there across the landscape, neatly painted with big wooden balconies they look peaceful, wealthy, idyllic.

Linz stands on the side of the Danube too, there's a huge free car park across the main bridge over the river. It's so hot, not a cloud in the sky, we need some shade but can only find a small tree to park next to. Not enough cover for the middle of the day so we walk over the bridge into town. Red and orange banners and posters everywhere advertising the festival, in it's 27th year, a photograph of a guy balancing a crystal ball on his head, the streets guaranteed to fill with thousands and thousands of visitors.

We sit under umbrellas at one of the cafes that line the edge of the main square, imagining the transformation. This big plaza, calm and slow today in the afternoon sun, flooded with the crowds that'll be here over the weekend. Rattling our ice cubes, clinking our glasses, we wait for the temperature to cool down before we make our way back to the van.

We check in the next day, join the queue at the festival office in a University building in the main square. The young student staff in festival t-shirts greet us with enthusiasm, fresh faced, smiling, speaking perfect English. Artistes are turning up in large numbers, over 100 acts arriving from all over Europe, from other parts of the world too. Jugglers, clowns, acrobats, mime artists, fire eaters, puppeteers, magicians and musicians. Everyone's at the end of some long hot journey from a far-off place, all checking in, weary from travelling, tiredness mixed with the buzz of anticipation. Every stairwell and spare space in the building has become home to instrument cases, everywhere you look there are unicycles, double basses, sound systems, outlandish costumes, trolleys full of luggage. It's backstage vaudeville, the myriad of props and accessories needed to busk and entertain on the street, everyone commandeering their own bit of storage space. A mix of people, from tanned and bare-chested blokes wearing waistcoats to guys in suits and ties. From burlesque ladies and slight girls built for gymnastics to top hats, tie-dyed baggy pants and dreadlocks, sometimes a bit of everything.

Some of them are the circle acts that take centre stage and perform at the pitches in the main square. The circle acts are like rock 'n' roll stars, you can spot them, the ones with the extra confidence, the extra swagger. Theirs are the big shows drawing the big crowds, high adrenaline and high stakes, they have to attract an audience, entice them, impress them and keep them watching for the duration. When they do they stand to make a lot of money in the hat.

In the queue for checking in we're next to a young bleached blonde American who lives in a commune with her boyfriend in Berlin. She performs Marlene Dietrich type songs on an accordion, says it feels funny to be performing legitimately for a change. We see some familiar faces from the Italian festival we played a few years ago, Gadjo, a gypsy street band from Barcelona, they've just driven 2000 miles to get here in a second hand police riot van. Six of them and a baby, they remember us from Italy. I'm impressed they're still together and haven't split up given how closely they work together, busking full time on the streets of Barcelona. One of them says,

"We've just learned not to push each others buttons."

They're a festival in a band, high energy music, loads of theatre, they know how to draw a big crowd. Others acts are smaller, quieter and take the pitches in the side streets and walkways. These are the spots for us, we're given a number for when we can come in each morning and choose our three places for the day.

Accommodation is in a university hall of residence not far from the centre. A few sweaty trips to bring everything up to our room on the third floor and we have a home for three nights. It might only be a small student room but it feels like heaven, modern, clean and immediate access to a shower, we waste no time to get in it, then fall asleep in the afternoon with the windows wide open.

The city cools down in the early evening, all the artists come together for a big parade to signal the start of the festival. Everyone's in full costume, every kind you can imagine. Medieval, fantasy, comedy, velvet suits, striped stockings, big trousers held up by colourful braces and lots of painted faces. The ones that have got it, flaunt it. Stilt walkers towering over our heads, jugglers, unicyclists, drummers, brass bands, everyone's playing to the crowd. Four Belgian guys dressed as firemen are doing a slapstick routine near us, fooling with a ladder and bicycle, swinging buckets and blowing whistles. The people lining the streets love it, clapping and cheering as the crazy spectacle walks by. The circus has come to town, the party has started, the festival has begun.

We grab our gear for the first couple of spots. It's Thursday evening, they say the big days of the festival are Friday and Saturday but there's already a lot of people about. The organisers have allocated pitches randomly tonight, our first one is on a wide street corner, so much going on that people only stop briefly, the fear of missing something spectacular around the corner keeps the crowd moving.

The next pitch is much better, a quiet side street off the central plaza. As we make our way through a slim walkway the noise and commotion from the main square fades away. An audience start to gather, forming a semicircle around us, smiling at us as we set up, expectant. There's a bar close by, people sat outside drinking at tables. People stay for the whole show and throw a good amount of euros in the guitar case at the end. Drinkers from the tables at the bar come over and give too. We sell a bunch of CDs, it feels good tipping all the coins and notes into our money bag. I make a note of the pitch so we can choose it another time.

Breakfast the next morning is in the canteen of our halls of residence. You can tell it's a busker's breakfast, everyone eats enough for two, a high energy intake before showtime. At the buffet table I can see some of the artists planning a packed lunch, putting bread rolls, cheese and apples in their pockets for later.

One person from each act has to choose their pitches for the day. Jayne thinks I'd be better at this, being the navigator and all, I'm more of a map reader than she is. At the office there's a number system and every act waits in a queue. Lots of acts, waiting their turn or just hanging out, sleepy eyed, there's a barefoot guy walking around brushing his teeth.

A smiley member of the festival team calls out my number, shows me the wall charts, the available pitches and times. Her English is excellent, we talk earnestly about the pros and cons of the different options,

"I think you have made very good choices,"

she says, then tells me there's an option to play an additional spot late in the evening if your music isn't too loud. I take it.

"Good idea," she says, before saying good luck and have a nice day and calling the next number in the queue.

We have a small battery amp, it's not big but it's heavy, too heavy to carry. We're using a makeshift way of moving it around by putting it in a small wheelie suitcase. It doesn't really fit, it sticks out, the zip won't do up so we tie it on with a bungee lead. The suitcase tends to rock from side to side if it hits a little bump in the road, momentum sometimes tips it over, cobbled streets are a no go. We're also carrying our instruments and a mic stand in our hands, on our backs we put stuff like our CDs in a small rucksack. Other buskers are much more organised and have special trolleys and carts to wheel their stuff around. Our life would be so much easier if we had one.

Trailing our gear in the heat of the summer sun we bump into the blonde haired American woman from Berlin. She's in top hat and tails, wheeling a robust looking trolley without breaking a sweat, on her way to her first pitch of the day. We stop and admire her wheels and talk trolleys, she swears by hers, they sell them in the big DIY stores in Germany and Austria. The DIY stores are all out of town though, we'll have to wait.

By the evening the streets are crowded, huge crowds, thousands of people, hundreds standing in circles around each of the big acts. We have to cross the main square a few times when we move between pitches or go to the office. They reckon 200,000 people come to the city over the weekend and they'll all head for the main square first. The big fire acts, trick cyclists, the big steel structures for acrobatics and trapeze, so much choice for what to see.

There's a guy on his own with a guitar playing in the main square, nobody's watching, people just passing by. Why has he chosen that spot? I feel for him, feel for his solitary predicament, standing alone in the grand arena, dwarfed by the huge space and buzz of excitement in the other parts of the square. He's carrying on regardless.

Our extra pitch in the evening works a charm. It's by a large corner bar on a side street. The night is warm, everyone wants to be outside drinking, eating ice cream. The festival has officially finished for the day, we have a captive audience, they appreciate it, our money bag is really starting to get some weight to it.

On our way back at midnight we stop by an ice cream parlour, I dig out a handful of change from our bag and we sit outside on the tables in the street, watch the late night revellers making their way home. The parlour has a cool logo, a photo of the head and shoulders of a guy with a mohican made of black ice cream cones, his tongue out Mick Jagger-style, licking an ice cream. The place is called The Eisdieler, the ice dealer.

The parlour's getting ready to close, there's a

guy clearing up, wiping the tables and taking the chairs in. We recognise him, it's the man in the logo, the man in the big photo in the window with the ice cream cone mohican. We complement him on the great photo and his ice cream. He says he had to get drunk before the photographer took it, he was too nervous and self-conscious to do it sober,

"Wait a minute," he says, he goes back inside and brings us a key ring each. The photo in miniature on each one.

Over the weekend we walk miles around the city with our instruments, our makeshift trolley jolting and bumping along the pavements. Some streets get too busy to walk down so we learn the best short cuts and quiet alleys instead. Our legs ache and our feet are sore, our money bag of coins and notes getting bigger each time, feeling more and more like a swag bag.

At the festival office you can change up the coins with a big money machine they've got on loan from a bank. It's set up in a small secure side room, as we wait our turn I can hear a circle act changing their money inside, the sound of coins sliding into a steel funnel, the long clattering whoosh of metal against metal, clicking, chunking and counting. It seems to keep going for ages. I'm willing our bag of coins to make the same kind of noise but the machine takes half the time to total our earnings. Still, the money's returned back to us as brand new, clean, crisp euro notes.

The festival building also has a courtyard

and canteen where artists hang out in between shows. There's always something going on, jugglers practising, gymnasts warming up, someone taking a nap in the corner. Lots of bravado, lots of swagger, lots of neon wigs. We get talking to four street statues from Macedonia, they're all painted in white from head to foot, faces, hair, hands, costumes, everything, a white bicycle and guitar are leaning against the wall.

If you're chosen you get to play a show in a circus big top put up specially for the festival, The Kaleidoscope Tent. We're asked to play it on the final day, the early Saturday evening performance, a cross section of acts, a short show with a selection of what's on offer at the festival.

The tent is packed, about a thousand people, the atmosphere is electric and they lift the sidings up to try to cool it down. The audience cheer, clap, whistle and stamp their feet at the end of each of our three songs and we finish our last performance of the festival on a big adrenaline-fuelled high. From the wings we watch the last few acts and the show climaxes with an Italian clown performing incredible tricks with hats that sends the crowd crazy. Donations from the audience are shared amongst the performers and our money bag gets a final boost.

Sunday morning and the city is empty again, we want to linger, to preserve the festival feeling somehow. There's a Chinese restaurant doing a busker's lunch for 10 euros for any performers still in town, a few acts turn up but most have left, the weekend is over, it's time to leave.

Two weeks until our next festival, in a small village not far from Naples. An Italian woman saw us years ago, the sister of the man that runs the village festival. We got an email out of the blue asking us if we'd like to perform and how much we'd charge. Thought it would be a cool thing to do after Austria, the kind of thing we always wanted to do if we gave up our home, be able to leave one and make our way to another. We gave them an amount based on what Linz was paying, they agreed and we thought we could busk our way down in between.

At a big DIY store outside Linz we buy a trolley. Two proper wheels, two handles to push it along, like the one our blonde American friend had, like the ones you see delivery drivers with. No more unstable suitcase bumping along behind us threatening to tip over at any moment, everything now goes on the trolley, any pavement, alleyway or cobbled street is passable.

Just a few hours of Austria to drive through. The roads start to climb until we're up into the Alps, heading to the Italian border, endless tunnels cut into the mountains as we rise higher and higher. Once we're on the other side, across the border, we'll stop for our first macchiato coffee. One euro at the motorway services. Fuel for the van is expensive in Italy but fuel for humans isn't.

No real decision about where to go busking on the way, we keep debating it, too much choice but well known cities are out of bounds, you need licences for places like Florence and Venice. Maybe we could busk around the tourist spots at Lake Garda? Probably too busy, maybe we could go to Bologna, we spent some time there twenty years ago and know our way around a bit. Nothing's jumping out at us, so we keep looking at the map, rolling along the motorway, heading down through Italy until we get to Tuscany.

Lucca, I wonder what Lucca is like? Not far from Pisa, not far from the coast. A walled city and zooming into the map I can see the centre criss-crossed with pedestrian walkways leading from one piazza to the next, perfect for busking.

Late July and the weather's hotter here than in Austria. Looking at the map there's a small campsite in Lucca near enough to walk into town. It's coming up to midday as we're driving down a quiet little street, small caramel coloured apartment blocks, shutters half closed, balconies with flower pots, little hardy plants, clean laundry drying in the warm air. Past some allotments and a football pitch, the site is on the other side of a hedge along the road, through a security barrier by a small reception building.

The guy on reception is relaxed, taking it easy in the heat, says there's one spot left. We count ourselves lucky given the time of year and book in for a few nights. Bushes mark out each pitch, the trees on the outer wall keep us in the shade, way too hot in the middle of the day to go busking, it's siesta time and the shops are all closed anyway. They don't open again until around 4pm, things'll pick up in the early evening.

We wait until late afternoon, load our busking gear onto the new trolley and set off into town, towards the big city walls, ten metres high in some places, the imposing brick ramparts that still wrap all the way round the outside of the city. Grand gateways and entrances, our closest is Porta San Donato where two lanes of road merge into one through an archway, massive ancient iron doors, always open.

People are strolling in the passageways and piazzas around the centre, sitting drinking aperitifs outside cafes and bars. Locals and tourists, lots of them, every restaurant has tables and chairs on the street.

Where to go? We meander around until we find ourselves in a small piazza, it's walls the colour of mustard and burnt orange, a statue of Giacomo Puccini in the middle. The famous Italian opera composer was born here. There's a couple of bars in the square too, we figure with it's musical heritage they might appreciate us. We don't know of any busking regulations in Lucca, there was something online about permission at one spot in the main square but we don't look into it and don't ask about it.

In the changeover to using our new trolley I've forgotten to pack a microphone. Jayne isn't impressed, neither am I, we're both sweaty from walking in the heat. She says,

"Let's leave it tonight."

It's me that forgot it so I'll take the hit,

"Have a beer and I'll be back as soon as I can."

I take a quick march back to the campsite. Without the trolley I make the round trip in 25 minutes, Jayne's just finishing her beer, settled in and starting to think about having another one.

I've had more time to think and I'm apprehensive about playing, I always get nervous about what'll happen when we play on the street in a strange town. We're on the walkway that runs across the south side of the square, facing inwards to the passers by as well as those sat at the tables outside the bars. The thing is, we're uninvited, we're making noise in an unfamiliar place, it's a leap of faith, anything could happen, we might offend people or antagonise them. I can feel the flow of my breath like a bellows and my heart rate climbing, my body getting heavier. Maybe we'll get stopped before we even start or worse than that, maybe they'll just ignore us and we'll be wasting our time.

The heat of the afternoon has dropped a few degrees as it slips into early evening but the air has stayed warm. There's relief when we finish our first song, the people sat in the piazza give us a round of applause and their soft clapping echoes off the walls. That feels good, that seal of approval, my heart rate slows, it's like we're meant to be here. A waiter from a bar comes and asks us if we'd like a drink. We relax into it, the sound gently bounces around the high buildings that overlook the small square, some of the passers by stop, take a look and a listen to what we're doing then decide to sit and have a drink at one of the bars.

Lucca has a summer programme of concerts, big name international artists. We've seen large posters around town, only last night Neil Young was playing in a piazza in the city centre so we finish a set with one his songs, a romantic song for a romantic evening, 'Harvest Moon'. A group of three English people sat near us come over and put a five euro note in our case,

"Thank you, we waited all night for him to play that song but he never did."

They're from Swindon, have flown over for the concert. We talk about how beautiful Lucca is, wonder why it isn't a better known tourist destination. This beautiful, ancient city, a living museum, history you can still walk around. They take our details, say they'll look out for us back home if we're ever in Swindon.

The only cars allowed inside the city walls are police cars, one drives past, it slows down and both policemen take a sideways look at us then drive on. A bar owner comes over and asks if we'd like to come back tomorrow night.

So we get into a routine, the daytime's too hot to do much at all so we lie in the shade, consider the time well spent while the battery amplifier charges through the van's cigarette lighter, ready for the evening.

Around 5pm, the temperature's still high but we tell ourselves it's starting to cool down, motivate ourselves to get going. We load up the trolley, push it into the city and take up our place opposite the statue of Puccini. The waiter from the bar brings us a drink, we give our little evening concert, grateful for the euros that get dropped in the open guitar case, each one another endorsement for being in this place in this city.

I love looking up and around as we're playing, at the four storey buildings that hug this small historic square in a cosy embrace, up past the shutters on the windows, the old walls. Up to the night sky overhead turning darker shades of blue. Then back down again to the diners and drinkers sat at the little round tables under large cream coloured umbrellas. In the middle of the square, the big bronze statue of Giacomo Puccini sat with his legs crossed, one hand on either arm of the armchair, confident, relaxed, eyes straight ahead like he's watching us.

When we've finished playing we always end the night sat outside one of the pizzerias, the waiters happy to be paid with a stack of coins from our earnings, they can never get enough of the change. One of them notices our instruments loaded on the trolley, says if we think Lucca is busy now we should see it in November when there's an International Comic and Games Festival, he thinks we'd do well then.

Then back at the campsite in the late evening

we put the coins in piles on our table, count up the money and work out what we've earned. All the two euro coins we set aside for fuel, the smaller coins for everything else. Banknotes we put together with the money we earned in Linz, folded up in a thick brown envelope and tucked into a safe place, our fund for the winter. The sticky residue from handling coins turns the water black when I wash my hands, nobody else uses the shower block this time of night, just insects buzzing around the fluorescent lights. Our energy's all worn off and we climb in the back of the van, hot enough to leave the side door open while we sleep, maybe a bit of breeze will make it's way in and cool us down.

On the last morning, as we're getting ready to leave, the red light on the amplifier comes on, it's not charged up even though we've had it plugged in. It doesn't take long to realise the cigarette lighter in the front is only connected to the car battery, not the leisure battery. Everyday we've been charging it from the wrong one and the van won't start. We don't have jump leads, neither do the campers near us, turns out you can't bump start a diesel engine either.

The man in reception makes sympathetic noises but gestures that he can't help. Just as he's apologising, saying there's nothing he can do, a maintenance man in a van turns up outside. He has a handy look about him and when we ask, he has jump leads. So the guy in reception comes out and together with our neighbouring campers we all stand in a semi-circle around the maintenance guy as he starts us up. One man doing the job, a small crowd gathered round to watch. He says we should run the engine for an hour or so to top the battery up. No problem we say, we're heading down to Naples, over five hours away.

We decide to take a trip down memory lane and go to Sorrento, it's not far from our festival at the weekend. Twenty years ago we spent a summer holiday there and have some great memories. Memories of the rustic campsite set up on a hill overlooking the Bay of Naples, Mount Vesuvius in the distance across the beautiful blue water. Other memories too like the tomatoes that used to float in on the tide as we drifted on a double lilo at the beach.

Back then we arrived in Sorrento by train but it's a totally different experience arriving by car. Dangerous winding coastal roads, hairpin bends, cliff edges, steep drops down to the sea, Italian drivers beeping horns, trying to overtake, honking that we're driving too slow. Of course we're driving slow, these roads are perilous. It's nothing like it looks in the movies, Jayne's gripping the steering wheel, cursing. There's nowhere to pull over either, we arrive at the campsite frazzled, try to put it out of our minds that the only way out of here is back along the roads we just came in on.

The campsite definitely isn't the same place it was twenty years ago. What were we expecting? We remember the kind family that ran it, the camaraderie of those staying here and the friends we made, did we imagine time would have stood still for two decades? The place has been renovated, there's a glass screen in front of reception now, the guy behind it is expressionless, doing his job, checking us in. Memory Lane has been bulldozed, knocked down to make way for a new development, whatever it is we don't like it.

Sorrento seems more touristy now too. We consider going busking, there are musicians and human statues in places around the town, after the drive and the disappointment we just don't feel like it.

We make a plan to leave early, do our best to avoid the traffic and busy roads on the way out, a clean getaway. It makes no difference, even at 6am the winding narrow roads out of town are still full of drivers trying to overtake, beeping their horns, waving their arms if they can't get past.

The festival we're going to is in a little hilltop village, not far from the town of Avellino. We've been promised basic accommodation and given the address of a farm stay. The road names in the hills are hard to follow, we're driving around and can't find the farm stay, we keep going past a huge three storey Roman villa. The whole estate is fenced off and has a security gate, the villa has a grand cascading staircase that flows down to fountains in the large grounds. Eventually we give up trying to find the farm stay and stop to ask for directions. There's a family standing outside a small house, one of the teenagers has a scooter, he says to follow him, he'll ride in front and show us where to go.

He takes us back to the huge three storey Roman villa, presses a button at the security gate, says something into the intercom. The gates open, he waves us in then turns his scooter round and waves goodbye. This is the farm stay, the long driveway curves up past the gardens and fountains around to a car park at the back.

Polite staff at reception welcome us, show us our room and say there's drinks waiting for us on the terrace. They take us to join two English guys sat at a table outside. Bruce and Jamie, they're in a jazz band, they're from Brighton and have flown over for the festival. The guys are young, good looking, charming and well spoken, shades propped up on top of their heads and dressed in loose white summer shirts, they seem used to drinking cocktails on hotel terraces. They're expecting the third member of the band to arrive soon, he's driving down in his sports car from England.

We start talking like old friends, things we have in common like music and gigs. Also Brighton, we lived in a bedsit there for five years. Their band's a proper professional outfit, The Swing Ninjas, they get all sorts of well paid work, corporate events, weddings and international festivals. The waiter brings more drinks, before too long we've got our instruments out and are playing music, swapping songs, the sun getting lower as the sky changes to darker shades of pink and blue. Lights come on in the grounds illuminating the fountains below, white lamps mark out the sweep of the long driveway as a red open top sports car comes through the security gates and makes its way up. The third member of their band has arrived.

A mini bus comes to the hotel and takes us all to a taverna for something to eat. Along with the other acts and the festival team we sit around a long table and are served several courses, local bread, pasta, tomatoes and basil, fresh buffalo mozzarella. There's around fifteen acts booked for the weekend. Organisers of Italian festivals always tell you about the food arrangements first, when we'll eat, where we'll eat, the local specialities and why theirs are the best.

Our friend Paulo is here. He's a one man band from Rimini on the west coast of Italy. Paulo plays the streets full time, all year round, summer and winter. He says with a wife and three children he has to, says he's thinking of going into Avellino tomorrow morning to busk but it might be too hot, even for him. We talk about the coming winter, what we might do, ask him about busking in Italy. He does it, it gets cold though. Sometimes he goes up to the German Christmas markets, it's even colder there. So cold that he only plays for fifteen minutes at a time before taking breaks inside cafes to warm his hands. He's made of tougher stuff than us, he's compact, fit, looks like an action man. We ask him about places in Europe he's been that he's played and enjoyed. He says he loved Denmark, he took his whole family there, busking all around during the

Danish summer holidays.

It's so hot around Naples this time of year, not much happens until the sun goes down. The festival starts in the evening, a big local event, all the neighbouring villages come out. Cars parked along the verges of all the roads leading up the hill into town, crowds of people making their way in. There are pop up cafes, canteens and kitchens serving food from big cooking pots. Market traders and street sellers too, they pitch up in the spaces in between, anywhere there aren't already tables and chairs.

As the street entertainment we're left to do our own thing. Play what we like, where we like, for as long as we want. There's a lot going on, market stalls, food and drink, every pop up kitchen is packed or has a queue. The locals walk by, looking at us as an oddity, strangers, like the carnival's in town. They're indifferent, not sure what to make of the street acts, not used to putting money in the cases of buskers either. By Monday we'll all be gone, life will be back to normal for them. We wheel our trolley around the town trying to improve each spot, hoping the next one will be better. Around one in the morning and the crowds have thinned out, people are heading home so we call it a night, our money bag not much heavier than when we arrived.

The next morning Jayne wakes up with a migraine. It was a long hot day yesterday, that might have caused it, she's done a lot of driving recently too, then there were the crazy roads in and out of Sorrento. Jayne doesn't get migraines often but if it's a bad one she can't even hold down a glass of water. Not only that, it can take at least a day or more to get better. It's the final day of the festival and we're due to play this evening. Our plan is to drive back to the UK tonight, straight after we've finished, in the middle of the night.

Jayne feels terrible and her temperature's going from hot to cold. One technique we learned for getting rid of migraines is to use flat cola, a couple of spoons every half an hour or so until she can eventually hold down a glass of water. We try this through the day but by late afternoon there's no sign she's any better. There's no way Jayne can play tonight.

I get Paulo's help in translating to the organisers that she isn't well, I tell them I'll play solo guitar instead, keep our side of the contract by providing some street music. They seem okay with that.

The streets feel even more distant tonight, even though the crowds are out in greater numbers I feel far away from everything, the people seem even more distracted. I keep wondering how Jayne is, is she any better, is there any chance of us leaving tonight? The Swing Ninjas walk past where I'm playing, stop to give me moral support, ask how Jayne's doing.

At the end of the evening we have to report to an office in town to get paid, I go in with Bruce from the Swing Ninjas. The office is full of paperwork, the main organiser is calling the shots, people following him around the room, heated discussions, drama, raised voices and arm gestures. Someone asks me for a company number for their records. I explain that Jayne and I are self employed and offer our national insurance numbers. There's more commotion, Bruce and I exchange looks, raising our eyebrows at each other, he seems calm though, flashes a reassuring smile like he's been in this situation before, he's experienced in Italian bureaucracy. The storm eventually blows over, they call me into a private room and hand over our money.

How is Jayne doing? I get back to our room but she's still not well, her temperature's all over the place, shivering one minute then overheating the next, the air conditioner's too cold but without it the weather's too hot.

We're in a predicament. It's Sunday night and there's this gig we've got in East Sussex on Tuesday night. This coming Tuesday night! Ridiculous I know, a small time gig to get back for. We'd emailed them a while ago asking about the flexibility of rearranging it but the reply came back that they wanted to stick with the original date. So we'd thought what the hell, we'll just set off from the festival late on the Sunday night, the ferry's booked for Tuesday afternoon. If we make a good start we'll be okay. One thousand two hundred miles, over eighteen hours of driving, that's not counting any stops, traffic jams or the slower speed that we drive at. Oh, and now the fact that Jayne isn't well, can barely stand up and hasn't eaten for over twenty four hours.

So it's the middle of the night on Sunday, we can't possibly set off and every hour that goes by shortens our travelling time. We're getting closer to cancelling the gig and saying we can't make it. Neither of us can sleep, we're drifting in and out, mostly awake, but around 5am Jayne sits up in bed and says,

"Let's try it, let's go."

I'm really not sure she's up for it. Jayne walks slowly to the van, gets in the driver seat while I load in our luggage. The sun's just coming up, another beautiful pink and blue sunrise, the air is cool this time of the morning. I set the satnav for Calais, twelve hundred miles away, and we head off through the hills around Avellino towards Naples and the motorway north. Quite how Jayne is doing this I don't know, something has kicked in and she's on a mission.

We stop every couple of hours for a macchiato and a croissant, each time we do she seems a little better. Is this a new recovery programme for migraine? Coffee and pastry. The miles roll by, the day rolls by, will we make it? It's Monday evening by the time we get to Switzerland, at the border they pull us over and charge us thirty euros for the privilege of driving through. The roads here are fast and clear, sweeping us past Lake Lugano, the sun has set but the moon is bright enough to light up the road.

On through the night. The satnav says ten

and a half hours to Calais, I'm sure it said that an hour ago, it's seemed to say that for ages, the time left doesn't seem to be going down. We decide we won't stop in Switzerland, just carry on through. Around 4am and we're in France, motoring up the east of the country, figure we should take some kind of rest, anything's better than nothing. We pull in, another services, another strong coffee, not as good as the ones we're used to in Italy but it should do the trick. Jumping in the back of the van we set the alarm for twenty minutes time, for when the caffeine kicks in. We lie out on the bed, fall straight to sleep, in a nanosecond the alarm goes off and we're back up, back on the road.

By 11am we're 70 miles from Calais, around an hour and a half to go. Confident that we'll get there we take the luxury of one hours sleep before driving to catch the ferry.

I can't believe it, we make it back to the UK in the afternoon but the adrenaline that fuelled the journey has completely worn off. We're exhausted, hardly any sleep, even when I stand still I feel like I'm moving. That strange feeling, a kind of jet lag, so tired that we daren't even take another nap, we know we won't wake up. How Jayne pulled that whole thing off I don't know, she likes a challenge.

Maybe the gig will revitalise us, give us the strength we need to get through the evening. It's in a little wine bar outside Eastbourne. Any chance of feeling energised disappears though, just a small handful of people having a quiet meal and a drink.

The owner comes up at the end and says,

"These Tuesday music nights aren't going so well, I'm going to change them to Fridays, give us a call about coming to play again."

5. ROLLING ON

My eyes open but they don't want to, reluctant, bleary, disorientated. I can tell from the light coming through the side of the curtains that the sun is high in the sky, it feels like the rest of the world would have woken up ages ago. Where are we? Parked up on a street for sure, I can hear footsteps walking by, a car going past. My body feels like lead, it comes back to me, the long, long drive, no sleep, parking up on a street close by the gig at the end of it. I remember as well that we've another one tonight, I better check the time. Midday, that's okay, all we've got to do is get to Canterbury this evening, a couple of hours away. Jayne's still sleeping, I set the alarm for three o'clock and close my eyes again.

Driving into Canterbury the roads outside give way to a city that was never built for cars. Small streets, some you can go down, some you can't, one ways, alleyways and pedestrian areas with different loading restrictions. The pub is right in the centre, no parking outside so we put the van as close as we can, about half a mile away, and load up the trolley. We're not thinking straight, we could've just dropped the stuff off then come and parked. The trolley's never felt so heavy, pushing it through the city feels like pushing it up a steep hill.

"Let's keep our expectations low, yeah?"

I'm giving a half-hearted team talk, talking to myself really, we're both tired, still recovering, trying to stay motivated. We'll just play some songs, earn some money and go home.

The pub is L-shaped with the bar at the short end, definitely the nicer end, the busy end, high tables, all of them occupied. Business people in suits, briefcases on stools or by their feet, after work drinkers, students and couples. The long side of the L-shape is much quieter, empty tables and chairs, windows looking out onto the street. We're playing down at this end, it's also where the toilets are.

When someone comes into our part of the bar we soon learn it isn't to watch us, it's to go to the toilet. An occasional couple or small group come and sit at one of the tables, Jayne and I exchange a glance, telling ourselves they've come to listen to us but they're mostly youngsters on a pub crawl, they have a drink and go. Occasionally a song resonates with the drinkers at the far end and we get a round of applause.

Then back up to Lincoln, a gig with some excitement, even some expectation about it. A hotel has just opened a bar in it's basement and is having events there. Suzie, the woman who does the hotel's PR, is in a league of her own. When Jayne's spoken to her on the phone, she's talked with a level of excitement that we're not used to. She's got an interview lined up for us on local radio as well as having done a load of other publicity, not only that, they've reserved a room at the hotel for us too.

We get to Lincoln around 1pm, the radio interview is at 3pm so we check in and meet Suzie. She's in reception, short straight blonde hair and a smart suit, smiley, carrying a clipboard. Just as excited in person as she has been on the phone, says that her and her team will all be listening in this afternoon. We can advertise the gig on air and the station want us to play a couple of songs live in the studio. Suzie has a full schedule this afternoon, but as it's only round the corner she'll walk us there.

At the radio station, glass double doors from reception lead to a small waiting area in a corridor, a couple of red square armchairs in front of the radio's logo. The afternoon show's already started, it's playing at a low volume in the background, big hits, 'Livin' La Vida Loca', 'Simply the Best'. We tune up the guitar and ukulele, sit in the red chairs, wait for the presenter to call us in. The corridor runs between the radio studio and a large open plan office, staff coming and going, the double doors to reception opening and closing.

An assistant comes to get us. The afternoon show's being hosted by someone standing in for the regular DJ,

"Thanks for coming in guys."

His head's turning from one computer screen to the other, then back again, a pile of paperwork on the desk, says we'll keep it simple, we'll play into the same mics we'll be talking into,

"Sometimes musicians play in the proper studio we've got next door."

The national news is on, then he says it's the local news and then we'll be live on air. The local news finishes, there's a jingle and we're on,

"Are you guys excited about your gig tonight?"

As Jayne opens her mouth to speak the presenter starts nodding, shuffling his paperwork and looking at the computer. I think he's trying to work out what to ask next.

"That went really well."

The hotel reception staff are all in agreement behind Suzie's shoulder. We go down to the basement, the underground bar's been newly renovated in the style of a 1960's night club. Smokey brown walls, peach coloured lampshades hanging from the ceiling, psychedelic pictures and leather seats. A great place for a gig and in the early part of the evening the place starts to fill up. Then people keep coming until the place is packed.

Suzie's all smiles and congratulations at the end, very happy with how it went. She gets people to write their comments in marker pen on one of our posters, asks us to sign it too. Suzie wants a memento to put up on the wall in the bar, people have been writing on it saying what an amazing evening they've had, how good we were. She says she'll have us back, we can arrange another date.

We drive back down to Kent, to Broadstairs on the east coast for a booking coming up on Sunday. We'll be early but there's a folk week just starting, maybe there'll be a lot going on, it's August and the height of summer.

The town is full to the brim with people. They're everywhere as we drive in, streaming past in their t-shirts, shorts and sandals, inches away from our windows when the high street narrows and the oncoming vehicles have to wait to pass. To the north of the town there's a long road that meanders along the cliffs. A mix of B&B's and residential properties, great sea views. We're up high, long steep steps lead down to the beaches, there's spaces further along the road, away from town. A little sign on a lamp post says no motor caravans overnight. There's a couple of other camper vans parked up amongst the row of cars, we should be okay to sleep here despite the signs. The houses are far enough back, it doesn't look like they'll be curtain twitchers.

We take a walk into town and bump into Bob, our salt and pepper bearded friend from Whitstable with an everlasting pocketful of change. He's come over on the bus for the music, invites us to go for a drink and fills us in on what's happening.

There are basically two competing factions at Broadstair's Folk Week. First, the official festival, folk concerts at venues in town for which you either pay for a ticket or get into because you've bought a pass for the week. Alongside, or as Bob says, up against this, every pub puts free music on all day, every day, to draw the crowds into their venue to drink beer. The music they put on is blues, rock and pop and they're all in competition with each other.

All around town are posters advertising the Folk Week but the music coming out of the pubs is anything but. It's a local musician's busiest time of the year, each pub needs to fill all it's slots for the day and bands go straight from one booking to the next, from one bar to another. Bob says goodbye to us, he's going to check out some more music, he only comes over during the day, by the evening it's all turned up too loud, people are too drunk. He'll see us around and might come again tomorrow for our gig in the afternoon.

We try to find out what folk events are on, the quieter, sit and listen type concerts. At the festival office in town I ask if there's a list we can look at, they say we have to buy a festival programme to find out. Maybe they could just tell us what's on today? No, we have to buy the programme. Walking back through town, the sound of rock and blues spills out onto the street from every bar. The town feels like the school prefect and the school bully have been locked in the same classroom.

The next morning we're woken by the sound of a seagull when it lands on the roof with a heavy thud. Then the patter of it's footsteps as it walks up and down. I open the sunroof and it flies away then light the camping stove to boil some water, the steam rising up and out of the gap. We arrange ourselves sideways on the bed with our coffee, half asleep, staring out to sea, the wind turbines far away on the horizon, seagulls circling over the green and grey water, dreamlike, peaceful. I feel tired, then I remember this time last week we were in Italy, just seven days ago, all those miles, three random gigs, another one this afternoon.

"I think it's time we booked our flights."

Jayne's right, she can't ignore and put off responsibilities like I can. We've been planning to go to New Zealand next February, some gigs in the diary. There's enough left in the bank account and to get a good deal now is about as late as we'd want to leave it.

At one of the hotels in town we buy a drink so we can use the wi-fi, open up the laptop and search for a good deal on flights. My finger makes little circles with the arrow on screen and hovers over the 'buy now' button. We take a deep breath. Done. We're going to New Zealand in February, the second half of our winter is sorted. All we've got to do is figure out what we're going to do for the first half of it.

The gig in the afternoon in Broadstairs is uneventful, just one of the many things going on as part of every pub's version of the festival. Halfway through our set I can see a musician bringing his equipment in, stacking it up in the doorway. He leans against the wall by his gear, watching, waiting for us to finish so he can set up and play himself.

We drive over to pick up our mail and stay the night with Shinina and Carlos. An evening of suburban comfort, a hot shower, a meal round a kitchen table, lying out on the sofas in their front room. All the things we gave up, they feel like luxuries when they're so temporary and we don't know when they'll come again. On a walk around the neighbourhood, Shinina's in her wrap around shawl, says she's restless and looking for adventure somewhere else. Carlos isn't so sure, he earns good money fitting high-end bathrooms, he doesn't like it but with the cost of living feels there isn't another choice. Shinina is certain there's a better life for them somewhere else.

They come to see us at our next gig, another pub, a midweek one in Whitstable. Busy with summer holiday makers, busy with seagulls too, trying to feed off the scraps of takeaway food filling the bins. The pub is crowded, the only space for the music is behind a pillar near the entrance.

After the gig some of the takeaways are still open, we get a bag of chips and sit on the sea wall. Where were we yesterday? I have to think for a minute, make an attempt at stitching our timeline together, the places we've been. The five gigs since we got back, distant memories, like they happened ages ago, weeks or even months ago.

When we turn up somewhere one of the first questions we get asked is where we've come from. We can't remember sometimes, pausing while we think about it. Jayne and I looking at each other quizzically, genuinely trying to work out where we've just been. It looks like we're being secretive, evasive, trying to hide something, we get a disbelieving look that says,

"Surely you must remember where you've just been?"

Time is different on the road, it bends differently, the gravitational pull of so many places stretches it, makes recent events feel further away. Much more so than when we lived in one place. Living in one place! That seems a lifetime away but it's only been two months.

We know where we're going next, Eastbourne, where I grew up. There's a cafe and restaurant on the beach that's started having live music early evening in the middle of the week, hoping to attract more customers when people are eating. The manager puts us in the large open space near the kitchen doors facing towards the entrance, all the dining tables are way over to our left and right. Behind us the busy doors to the kitchen are opening and closing, waiters and waitresses going in and out.

My mum and dad and their respective partners bring their friends along and they sit at a far table by the window. They make the kind of appreciative noise audiences make when a family member is performing, exaggerated cheering, longer rounds of applause than necessary. Other diners turn their heads to try to figure out what the fuss is about.

Tomorrow we've got a spot at a town festival in Falmouth in East Cornwall. A long drive so we pack up quickly, say our goodbyes, set off through the night. Jayne's got her all night mojo going and wants to keep driving but at 3am I persuade her we really need to stop. I know it won't play out well tomorrow if we miss too much sleep again so we pull over in a lay-by.

They've put up a small marquee in the square in the centre of Falmouth, some plastic chairs in front of a little stage. Friday afternoon, a slow start, we're playing to a few people walking past plus the soundman and the guys who are tuning up to play next. They pay us some travel expenses and tip us off about a good curry house in town.

The locals at the pub in Weston-in-Gordano have persuaded the landlord to have us back. It's only two months since we were there, on our first week on the road, it feels like last year. I'm not sure if the pub's making much money when they have live music but the huddle of locals that come along like it, there's a lot of drunken banter. Paul brings his harmonicas, him and Aileen say to come and stay with them next time, they say we'll be in trouble if they find out we've driven past on the motorway and not stopped to see them. If we can get a few more of these regular bookings we could make this whole thing work.

On a trip to the west country earlier in the year, before we'd sold up, when the money we earned went on accommodation, we'd gone busking to make ends meet. We went to Taunton, it was market day and we thought we'd found a good spot on the pedestrian street near the stall holders. No sooner were we ready, just before we were about to play, when a vehicle came along that needed to get in behind us, to the garage door we'd unknowingly set up in front of. Our first time in town, a little nervous anyway, embarrassed at having to move with the stall holders all looking at us, we were already off to a bad start.

We moved, put ourselves ten feet further down the street, tentatively played our first song. A tall lady in a smart brown coat came straight towards us, with purpose. Uh oh, I thought, the games up, we're in trouble now. But we weren't, quite the opposite, she said she'd like our details. Her and her husband have garden parties, would we be interested in playing one? How much would we charge? They have little get-togethers, invite a group of friends over for a concert, the last one they had was an Elvis impersonator.

So here we are in a residential suburb of Taunton, on a sunny Sunday in August, pulling up in Pauline and Ian's driveway to play in their garden. They're generous hosts, have laid out a large buffet, a big drinks table with wine, beer and a summer punch. The garden is full of tables and chairs set out for guests, a small gazebo has been put up to shade us from the sun, they've run a cable across the neat lawn for us to plug our gear in. As we're setting up, every now and again, they come and check everything's okay and tell us how well the previous party went, the one with the Elvis impersonator. It feels like a hard act to follow, every time they mention it Jayne takes a bigger sip of the summer punch they put in her hand when we got here.

The guests arrive, all stepping into the garden through the sliding doors at the back of the house, filling their plates and glasses from the big buffet then sitting at the tables expectantly.

We play our set, I can see their faces staring back at us, hot and shiny in the afternoon sun. I have no idea what they're making of it, the audience sipping their drinks, eating their sandwiches and sausage rolls, polite applause after each song. Are they enjoying themselves? Do they like it? I wonder what they were expecting after the last concert here with Elvis. Afterwards Ian takes us into the kitchen to have a quiet word,

"It's going well, could you do an extra half an hour?"

Sometimes an exchange of emails can be at such irregular intervals that we think a booking is

never going to come off. Everything goes quiet from the other side for ages, maybe after they've asked us what we'll charge and we've sent them our reply. The forthcoming silence we take as a 'no' and worry that we've probably got our fee wrong, try to let it go. A festival in Croatia played out like this. An email or two at the beginning, sounding positive, then months went by, nothing. All of a sudden there's a message in the inbox, are we still available? Do we want to come to Croatia? Why not, just the kind of situation we've dreamed of taking advantage of.

So we're going to Croatia, a festival in Varaždin, as street artists playing around the city, a week long event.

Since we've been busking more this summer we're thinking we could do with increasing our visual impact, something extra to make a statement and draw a crowd. We've got some outdoor fairy lights and figure if we can attach them to the frame of an umbrella, tie it to our upright trolley and plug them in this might do the job. So we strip the material off an old umbrella and cable tie the lights all around the framework. A big battery and an inverter gives us the power supply and this goes in a retro suitcase so we can tidy up the look of it. The case is heavy but when it's switched on it looks great.

Driving across country to the ferry in the early evening, we're waiting for the twilight and when it comes we pull over, jump over a gate into a field, set up a tripod and take a photo of ourselves under the umbrella with our instruments. Us with a starlight canopy, the sky dark turquoise and the little lights on the umbrella twinkling. We're pleased with ourselves, our idea and our new prop.

Once we're over the channel the drive to Croatia seems easy, we're not in a hurry, travelling in the daylight hours and resting overnight. Mostly German and then Austrian motorways again, stopping and sleeping in the service areas. After Austria there's a bit of Slovenia to pass through.

Slovenian roads are modern, fast and empty, we pass service areas under construction, slip roads that lead into building sites but nobody's working on them.

There's a security checkpoint on a small country road at the border to Croatia. No other traffic around but we have to wait at a red light for a while. When the light eventually goes green we drive up to the booth, stop in front of the barrier. The guard takes a long serious look at our passports, his head down, the silence lasting ages. It's not for us to break it either so when he looks up we're both peering back at him, straight faced and serious too.

Once we're through Jayne says,

"Let's try a Croatian coffee."

We stop at the first town and park up on the main street,

"What's the currency? Do they use euros?"

I don't know, I take out our euro purse and go into a cafe. On the menu on the back wall I can see the word 'Kava' at the top, that must mean coffee, I point at it and hold out some euro coins. The guy behind the counter shakes his head. I go back to the van,

"No they don't."

The currency is the Croatian Kuna. Varaždin is not far from the border and it's beautiful. Grand architecture, Austrian influences, clean, wide pedestrian streets, open spaces and town squares. At the festival office they use a two way radio to locate a member of staff to help us, send us out to a YMCA about a mile from town, give us a pass to put in the front window of the van so we can drive back in and park when the festival is on.

Friday evening, the city streets are busy, really busy, football match busy. People are out en masse wearing the glow-in-the-dark plastic necklaces and bangles that you only see at carnivals and festivals. I'm thinking our umbrella lights are going to look great here, surely giving us an edge in the middle of all this commotion. At least get people looking our way, draw some attention, maybe it'll make us some more kuna.

On a crowded thoroughfare amongst the bars and streets sellers we find a pitch, open up the umbrella that's now tied to our upright trolley and switch the lights on. They look good. No sooner have we begun than there's loud beeping from the battery, it's flat and about to run out. We've never tried it longer than a minute or two. I can't believe it! We have to switch the lights off and play in relative darkness.

The crowds are moving in opposite directions in front of us, flowing in and around each other. A sea of people streaming along, passing us by. We're lost amongst it all but then a teenage girl and her mother notice us and stop to watch. They're smiling, particularly the young girl, they both stay fixed in one place listening to our whole set oblivious to the world weaving around them. When we stop they come forward, the mother can't speak English but her daughter is fluent. She's twelve or thirteen, braces on her teeth, large glasses and straight brown hair, enthusiastic about our music to the point of having a tear in her eye. Wonderful, she says, her mother smiles and approves. They buy an album and ask us to sign it. They want to know where we'll be playing again over the weekend, we say somewhere on the streets of Varaždin. She says they'll look out for us but we don't see them again.

The festival are using a side room at a restaurant for the street artists to come and eat between shows. Croatian food turns out to be tasty and we pile up plates with fried potatoes, green beans and salads. We sit with a couple of friendly women from the Netherlands, good natured, attractive, long brown hair. Karin and Arlette, they have a street act, The Mobile Sewing Company, they make colourful alterations to people's clothing with a bicycle powered sewing machine. Both are tired after a long day travelling and delays at the border. Arlette didn't bring her passport thinking she didn't need it for mainland Europe. They had to phone home, get a copy emailed over, then someone at the festival office had to sweet talk the security man at the border. If he looked at it anything like he looked at our passports he must have stared the hell out of that photocopy.

The next day it's raining. Saturday should be the big day but the streets are deserted. The festival staff are down hearted, shaking their heads, checking phones for up to the minute weather reports. We wait around with our rain coats on, our trolley covered with a bin bag ready for action at a moments notice.

When the rain eases a little, a small number of people start to come into town. To show willing we ask one of the pop up beer sellers if we can play under his small shelter. This goes down well with the organisers and scores Jayne an early afternoon beer.

On a break at a cafe four people at the next table are smiling at us. We nod back, say a tentative hello. They keep looking over like they know us. There must be some mistake, then one of them says,

"Good to see you again."

I don't know what he means, I can't place them, he carries on,

"Did you like Linz?"

I look at their faces, a little closer, there's something familiar about them. Then I paint them from head to toe in white, obvious now that it's the street statues we met at Pflasterspektakel, the busking festival in Austria. The off duty, civilian versions, unrecognisable when they're unpainted and in plain clothes. We switch to their table and talk festivals. They tell us about a Macedonian one but warn us against it, not every agreement is honoured, not everyone keeps to their word.

On the way to our next pitch we catch Karin and Arlette performing, a crowd has gathered in a circle around them. They're wearing embroidered scarlet red dresses, red lipstick, red head scarves with flowers in their hair. They have vintage bicycles with umbrellas attached, sewing machines in old wooden cases and a record player. Arlette is pedalling one of the bicycles, powering a sewing machine that Karin is using to transform an item of clothing. An item of clothing that a member of the audience was wearing just a few moments ago, one they've given up for alteration, a whirlwind of activity as it's revamped before their eyes. A new design, fancy patches and buttons, frilly trimming, lace and embroidery. All the while Karin and Arlette are bantering with the audience and the volunteers, high energy sewing, the crowd love it.

On the last day we go to the office to get paid. They say that due to finance regulations in Croatia and in order to transfer our funds they need a particular form from our Inland Revenue, a special form for dealing with Croatia. Either that or they can just pay us in cash in euros. What the hell were we thinking when we said,

"No problem, we'll email our accountant and he'll get the form."

Our accountant hadn't heard of the form but wrote to the Inland Revenue. They wrote back that they hadn't heard of it either. Two months later and the festival just bank transferred the money anyway. We paid £40 for each of the letters the accountant wrote.

Another thousand mile drive back to the UK, not such a hurry this time, stopping overnight on motorway service stations. At one of them a German lorry driver's playing basketball, he's got a hoop fixed high up to the back door of his big truck. When I go to get something out of our boot he waves me over. A middle aged wiry guy wearing an old blue vest and a headband, he's working up a sweat bouncing the ball around and firing it at the net. We can't talk much, neither of us speak each other's language but I gather from him gesturing with a throwing motion, flexing his arm muscles, that it's keeping him fit. The ball bounces noisily off the tarmac and the back of the truck as we run around the car park passing it to each other, stopping every so often to let an HGV drive past.

Jayne suggests we go to Bruges for my birthday, I can eat waffles, she can drink Belgian beer, it's only a couple of hours to the ferry from there. We arrive at the outskirts late at night, into the early hours of the morning. No traffic on the road which is why I notice a car's headlights in the mirror, they seem to be following us. Whichever way we turn, they turn. Am I being paranoid? It's not a police car, that much I can see. I tell Jayne to do a u-turn and go back the way we just came, let's see what the car behind us does. They do the same, taking a u-turn too and following us. Now I'm spooked, we both are. What do we do? We turn around again and carry on driving back toward the city, accelerate and try to put some distance between us. On a wide street with parked cars along both sides we pull into a space. They drive by. We sit there. Now what? After a while we climb in the back, it takes ages to fall asleep.

We cross the channel back to Dover and drive

up to a pub in Shropshire. A big pub, the kind with hard floors, mahogany tables and chairs that make a screech when you get out of your seat. They have music on Friday nights. It's a quiet one, just us playing, a couple of families having an evening meal and the sound of the chairs scraping on the floor when someone gets up to go to the bar or the toilet.

We're not far from Shrewsbury and think we'll try busking there the next day, Saturday morning. Given how busy it could get and in order to get a pitch we'll go in early.

At 9am there's already people in town. On the main pedestrian street we go looking for an empty shop we can play in front of. There's one but it's already taken by a guy about to do a juggling act, we've missed out on a prime spot, we're too late. We walk up and down a few times looking for alternatives but can't see any, we're starting to get aimless, starting to lose motivation and momentum. Ten minutes later, the juggler starts to pack up, he's going, we don't know why and don't care, we jump into his spot.

Eleven o'clock is about as busy as it gets on a Saturday morning, we're getting a good collection of £2 and £1 coins. I grab a small handful of them, we take a break so each of us can go and find a loo and I can get us a coffee. By about 1pm we've played every song we know, a few of them twice, there are flurries of generosity from passers but lulls too, at some point we're going to run out of energy. We encourage each other to do one more session, a final push, goad each other to do another half an hour or six songs or something. You never know what might happen. We make it to 1.30pm but that's it now, we're tired and hungry. As we're putting the instruments away a guy comes up to introduce himself and say hi. He runs a coffee shop in Oswestry and puts on some music evenings and thinks we'd fit in, we swap numbers and agree to stay in touch, worth playing the extra half an hour. Then as we're walking away up the street, a young woman stops us and puts a £1 in Jayne's hand,

"I didn't have any change when I passed you earlier."

We thank her and drop it in our money bag, tipping some of it out a few minutes later to buy sandwiches. Back at the van, over at the edge of the car park, we help clean each others hands before we eat. Taking it in turns to pour from a bottle of water while the other washes their hands until the dirty water runs clear.

Over in Suffolk, there's a pub with a history of music and song that goes back decades, The Ship Inn, Blaxhall. Alan Lomax, the folk music historian, the guy who took field recordings of traditional music across America and the British Isles, made recordings at The Ship Inn in Blaxhall in 1953. Jayne found the place researching gig opportunities in the area and came across a BBC short film from 1955, old black and white footage in the bar, the residents stood around, tankards in hand, singing folk songs.

The pub's on a country lane just wide enough for one vehicle, it's side wall edges out onto the road as if to say I got here first and the road squeezes to accommodate it. Jayne's spoken to the manager a couple of times, he seemed pretty straight talking, a no nonsense kind of guy. When we get there Adrian's behind the bar, he's a big guy, bald head, round face, a meaty handshake, genial and welcoming. He runs it with his partner Siggi. It's more than a full time job, there's a B&B at the pub too, up first thing serving breakfast and working through until last orders. There's a glazed look in his eyes like he's working too hard.

It's late afternoon when we start playing, people are lingering at the end of Sunday lunch plus there's the regular drinkers, the ones that look like they never leave. At the back corner of the bar there's a table of old guys drinking from their own tankards, grey beards, walking sticks, arms folded, I don't know what they're making of us. The windows are open, the outside smokers and drinkers can hear us on the patio.

Adrian says he knows the guy who runs the big folk festival in the area, he's sent him a message to see if he's free to come down and take a listen. We finish our set, there's no sign of him so we pack up and go and sit with Siggi in the other bar. She has five dachshunds and brings them from upstairs to meet us. With the dogs jumping on us, competing for space on our laps, a guy walks into the bar, Adrian brings him over,

"Let me introduce you to John, he runs the festival."

He's too late to see us play but what's left to the imagination might be better than the real thing! John seems persuaded by Adrian and Siggi's testimonial, says to send him an email, Jayne asks,

"What's the best one, the one that'll get a response?"

She knows the festival email will get hundreds and hundreds, might as well throw a needle in a haystack. She also knows because she's already sent them a stack of emails. John gives us his private email.

Blaxhall isn't far from the sea. Up the coast there's a campsite near Sizewell B, the nuclear power station. The site's just back from the beach, you can either pitch in the open or take shelter by the trees at the edges. Early September now, schools have started again, the summer holidays are over. A few retired couples in larger camper vans, we put ourselves under one of the trees, it feels more homely.

We sweep out the floor, tidy up, take showers then cook a meal. In the early evening we play through some songs we're working on but stop just before the sun sets, so much earlier now, the dark evenings have crept up on us, just a little before 7.30pm tonight. Autumn and winter are on their way, it's the first time we've really noticed.

The weather's good at the moment though and the next day we take a walk along the coast. A track that leads through wild grass at the edge of where the shingle beach starts, a track that runs past old gun placements and hideouts until we end up in a pretty town. A picture postcard town. Thorpeness, beautifully painted colourful wooden houses, hanging baskets and picket fences. This is no ordinary town, it's too perfect, a pretty boating lake, pristine rowing boats waiting at the water's edge. Turns out to be the vision of a wealthy Scot who made his money in the railways and built a fantasy town for him and his friends. We come across a nice looking cafe and gallery that has a few music events, they tell us to email them about a booking.

Walking back along the path to the campsite, from Thorpeness up to Sizewell, herring gulls gliding overhead. On a sunny day like today the whole coast is dreamlike, the nuclear power station, a giant white golf ball luminous in the sunlight makes it more surreal. We email the cafe a few times but never hear anything back, there's a lot of gaps in next years diary still to fill.

We need a plan, winter's coming in like the tide, coming whether we like it or not. The best one we can come up with is to take the ferry when the clocks go back next month, make our way to Italy, busk there hoping that the weather holds out, maybe go to Lucca for the comics and games festival, try out other places too. Try to cover our costs

ADAM PIGGOTT

and add to the euro fund we've built up, trust that it'll see us through the rest of the winter. When it gets too cold, which it will, we'll drive across and down to the south of Spain and camp, we've just got to get through to February. Then we can make our way back for our flights to New Zealand, it'll be late summer in New Zealand then. That's the plan anyway.

We pack up our home again and drive the short distance to the Orwell Crossing Truck Stop, Karl has booked us for another gig. Mike the security guy is here, it's like we're old friends, Karl too. It's about the same as it was last time, just a few people. Still he says we can come again. Can they really afford to have music, how long can they keep this going? Is it just us, are the other nights much busier? We don't know. It's a dilemma playing these kinds of gigs, then being offered another one, what should we do? Someone's going to play it if we don't.

Up to Lincoln for Friday night. There's a pub right next door to The Strugglers, we asked the landlady Anna if it mattered to her if we played next door as well? No, she said they have a different crowd.

They definitely have a different crowd tonight. It's the Lincoln Steampunk Festival this weekend and the pub is their designated meeting place. Full of people dressed in Victorian costumes reimagined through a sci-fi lens from the future. Beards, monocles and moustaches, flying hats and goggles. It's a small pub, we're squeezed into a little corner by the back door, at the end of a slim section of the bar. Always comings and goings, people making their way in and out to have cigarettes. There's a Victorian sense of decorum, men doff their top hats and bowlers to allow ladies first or let each other pass. Well mannered, well spoken and appreciative, they make for a good audience. There's a polite bookishness, a punky nerdiness, a few of them say our music and style fits in well with the Steampunk aesthetic.

From Lincoln over to the Midlands. A cafe that puts on proper music events, the type where you're not just playing while people are drinking or eating. The kind where an audience pays a ticket price then sits and listens. We played here before a couple of years ago, we drove up specially, it was quite a success, nothing to do with us, we were the first on, two other acts after us with a bit of a following. It's in a community cafe in a ground floor space of a larger building, a pop-up art gallery upstairs. A funky vibe, posters on top of torn posters on the wall, it felt like a happening. It was so full, some of the audience had to stand. The kind of night where the audience and the artists hang around for ages afterwards drinking, talking, revelling in the afterglow of a good night. There wasn't a lot of money in it but it was such a great evening that Jayne had been writing to them ever since trying to fix up another date. Must have been a year later when they finally came through with one.

This time it couldn't be more different,

numbers are way down, the promotion's casual. Just a handful of people turn up, a single handful that is. Such a small audience that they're more self conscious than we are about it. Torn posters on the wall are no longer a cool background to a funky venue, just a sign that we're the last ones left in a forgotten building, faded, worn out and run down. Not even the smell of home cooked food this time, not worth it with such few people they say, just a big serving of humble pie and a small pocket of change for payment.

One constant, an easy going young guy who helps out there, Dan the bicycle repair man. Only in his twenties but with a much older head on his shoulders. He knows we're not from the area, at the end of the night he says if we'd like to we can crash on his floor. That gesture means a lot to us, that kindness, particularly tonight. We thank him but say we carry a bed of our own with us now, if we'd have thought it'd be more comfortable we'd have gone for it.

On a nearby side street we climb into the back of the van. The rolling side door always needs a big push to close it properly. I slam it once we're inside, hoping it shuts out more than just the world outside. It takes time to shake off a gig like that, shake off the feelings. Foolishness, worthlessness, false expectations dumping us on the other side of a hedge we've been thrown over rather than dragged through. Trying not to take it personally. Why can't we let it go sooner? What's the point playing gigs where no one's listening or where no one turns up?

We wake up the next morning to the sound of rain, heavy drops falling on the roof, metallic and loud. Windy too, rocking the van from side to side. A text message on the phone says the outdoor charity event we're due to play today is cancelled. We stay under the duvet and watch movies, the volume turned up against the noise of the rain.

Then south, the outer edges of our old stomping ground, old bookings that aren't too difficult to get. Maidstone, a pub on the outskirts run by Lee and his wife, we've driven over here and played a couple of times before. Lee's a friendly guy, reminds me of a sports pundit, average height and build, like a boxing coach or darts player. He loves music, crazy about it, plays the bass and the guitar, likes to join in whenever he can. There's music all the time, rock, blues and ska bands along with karaoke and open mic nights. A big pub too with a restaurant. The sort of place that can handle large crowds like birthday parties and funerals.

Most of the eaters and drinkers drift away through the evening, they're not really here for the music, maybe it keeps them for one more drink, some of them are only just getting started before they head into town.

A young woman comes in, long dark hair, wearing a black leather jacket on top of a colourful dress. She sits at the table in front of us,

"I watched one of your videos, it was good."

Maxine. All upbeat and smiles, immediately a

friend,

"I put the word out, no one else was up for it."

We chat to her in between playing songs. She's a singer too, plays gigs around town, suggests some venues to us. Nobody else is really listening or watching. Lee the landlord comes over, sits with Maxine for a drink.

Later on Shinina and Carlos turn up too. That's three people here to see us, our own little posse of supporters, they end up sitting together, they get on well with Maxine, everyone does. They give her a lift home at the end, we follow behind them, back to their place to stay over for some home comforts.

Sunday in Lewes, East Sussex, at the Conservative Club at the top end of the high street, in a regency building past all the shops. Playing in the bar in the afternoon, there's never that many people that come along. The staff put out a big plate of cheese and biscuits, it's on a table not far from where we play. During the first half the few punters come and help themselves, by the time we finish our first set it's nearly all gone.

Shirley comes if she's in town. She's retired, has a lifestyle that follows the weather, a home in New Zealand that she goes to in the winter. Next year she'll be back in England by the time we get there. Always asking if we've got a new album and writing to the club to get them to book us again.

Then up to The Smack in Whitstable again, we know the score with this one, the last watering hole in town, the last of the Sunday drinkers, the nearby car park we can sleep in. However Mike and Jeanette come to see us, the couple we met at the little campsite on the Isle of Sheppey, where we sat round the fire talking music. They offer us a space on their driveway to sleep the night. After the gig we follow them the short distance to where they live, Mike waves us in, manoeuvring us through their front gate to a parking space behind their camper van.

Their house is on the beach. They take us upstairs to a long glass fronted room, a kind of conservatory, they want to show us the view. It's midnight, the best view is with the house lights off, so Mike flicks the switch and we sit in darkness looking out to sea, drinking tea and eating toast. The Thames Estuary, the blinking lights of oil tankers, fishing boats on the water. Ahead you can see across to Southend, over to the left is the Isle of Sheppey. It feels like we're in a lighthouse with the wide panoramic views over the channel.

In the morning Mike wants to take us to a place that does a great breakfast, he's raving about it but it's not open on a Monday,

"Maybe another time," he says, and makes more tea and toast for us all to take upstairs for the view.

An unusual thing happened with our next gig, in Deal, on the other Kent coast. When the pub changed hands, the new owner phoned us about doing a gig. He phoned and asked us! This doesn't happen, well maybe once in a blue moon. Musician's say things like,

"I've been asked to play at _."

"We've been invited to perform at _."

Well, it's not true, at least 99 per cent of the time. The only way you get gigs is by repeatedly contacting people, knocking on doors, making enquiries, asking, then asking again. Nothing gave me more of an appreciation of this than when Jayne stopped ringing people for gigs with a band we used to be in, the gigs dried up straight away, within a short space of time the diary went blank, there was nothing in it. Nothing. Like falling off a cliff. Doesn't matter how good you are, you're gone, forgotten, forgotten unless you remind the world that you exist.

So the phone had rung, the guy had said he'd taken the pub on, was looking for acts, found our number from a list of bands that had played there before. He asked what we charge? Jayne asked what he could pay, he said what the most was, a very generous pub rate,

"That's absolutely fine."

The pub's on a residential one way street, terraced houses, single file traffic and single file pavements, if it wasn't for the sign swinging by a window on the second floor you'd miss it. The new landlord's a big tall guy, a six foot six Londoner, a great spade of a handshake. Talks like a cockney barrow boy, drops h's like a market trader and has the same intuition for good business. Every

Wednesday a burger truck does food in the back yard whilst the bar serves the booze to it's thirsty customers. It's cosy too, the ceilings hung with dried hops, music seems to add to the occasion. All sorts of people come along, it's a popular night, the pub attracts a range of random punters. It was the same even before it changed hands, you never know who you're going to meet. One night we met the production team of a Sky TV drama, a university professor specialising in self-harm and Tracey Emin's brother.

Sybil comes to see us when we're in Deal. Retired, sprightly and energetic, silver hair cut in a bob, well dressed and manicured. Always a sparkle in her eye and a smile on her face, even more so tonight as she's fallen in love and come out with her new boyfriend Ken. They're giggly, she introduces us to him, they can't take their eyes off each other, no use having a conversation, they're not listening to a word anyone else says.

To the west of the town are some quiet streets by the beach where we can park and stay the night unnoticed. Wake up to a sea view then take a long walk along the prom. It always seems to be windy in Deal. We walk into it first, save the feeling of propulsion for the way back, there's a place on the seafront we want to call into, we've been trying to get a gig there for ages. Run by a group of young guys, they've built a reputation for quality live music, particularly original music. Their website has the usual contact email address and suggests that acts and bands get in touch and send them a message. We've sent an email via the website, written to them a few times but never had a response.

We wait for it to open and go in to see them. One of the guys that runs it is there, he's nice, very polite. Seems interested in us and what we do, maybe talking face to face will do it, the personal touch. He suggests we send an email via their website.

Up to Cambridgeshire, a pub by the canals. Jayne rung them, one of those conversations you're convinced they're not interested and don't want to book you but at the end of the call they ask what dates we're available. Maybe we've made their life easy, they've said if it's busy they'll pay us a bit extra.

It's not that busy though. We're playing in an area that's down a few steps, lower than everyone else in the bar. Below the level of the few casual drinkers, diners finishing off fish and chips, looking over the banisters at us.

Behind the bar, the family that run it take it in turns serving, they stand with their hands behind their backs, step forward when a customer comes up, then return to their place when they've finished. The pub's on a canal, attracts narrow boats that are passing by, the boat owners we speak to say they mostly move on to avoid mooring fees. A man follows me to the toilet and utters inappropriate drunken profanities under his breath whilst I'm stood at the urinal. Later at the bar one of the family members steps forward to pay us and implies we could get another booking. We'll probably take it.

Some friends of ours are in a five piece band that busk in Norwich. The He Hews, this Sunday they're playing in a local pub, we thought we'd try busking in town in the morning then go and see them.

Even on Sunday the centre of Norwich is full of musicians. There's a main pedestrian street next to the market square. In the biggest pitch of them all is the full time busker, the local legend Jonny Walker, a young guy in a wide brimmed black hat, shoulder length hair, big scarf and flared trousers. A small crowd sitting watching on steps nearby. Press cuttings that he's got over the years are pasted on boards by his guitar case. Somehow I'm friends with him on Facebook but he wouldn't recognise me. I wrote to him recently about busking in France, he wrote back with some kind advice.

We walk up and down with the trolley. There's too much competition on the main drag, that's what we tell each other anyway. Shy today for some reason, not confident at all. Sometimes we just don't want the world looking at us, so we go down a side street, play for an hour or so on the crossroads of two pedestrian alleyways. Corners can be good, catching people going in four different directions, it's not a great pitch though, we've hidden ourselves away really. When we empty the guitar case there's probably enough to pay for parking and a drink this afternoon.

The He Hews are friends we met at Ferrara Buskers Festival in Italy a few years ago. We were the only two invited English acts. 'Invited', there it is, the word that implies it was them that called us. We applied to play there, so did The He Hews. All of us had taken time off our regular day jobs to spend ten days in a beautiful Italian city playing music on the streets. Hotel paid for, good food, earning money too. Hot sunny days, pizzas, ice creams, after show parties, we got on famously, had the time of our lives. The He Hews were dressed in pyjamas for the whole festival.

Trombone, tea chest bass, saxophone, snare drum and banjo. The He Hews play any music they want, reggae, jive, 1920's jazz, the theme from The Magnificent Seven, Amy Winehouse. They're the love children of the Bonzo Dog Doo Daa Band and Screaming Lord Such, Monty Python as close relatives. It puts a smile on everyone's face, makes you happy, makes you want to dance.

They're going down a storm when we arrive, people dancing in front of the stage. Johnny makes it swing with the snare drum, he shakes his head when he sees us, can't believe we've walked in, gives us a massive smile. At half time he's straight over with a big hug and immediately we're reminiscing about Ferrara. Jayne and I have been in a couple of good time bands. Whenever we see The He Hews we get nostalgic for it, people up dancing, revelling in the joy of the music.

We need a new battery for our busking amp, just in case it doesn't last out the winter. They're not something you can buy off the shelf either, quite specialised, only a few places sell them. Heavy too, I don't fancy our chances of trying to get one in Europe if we suddenly had to.

We're heading to the west country, there's a place that sells them on the way. A small warehouse on a red brick industrial estate, numbered units, a reception area attached to the main building. The air is cold in the waiting room, I ring a bell on the counter for service. A young man in a lab coat comes out, greased back hair, serious, asks what I want. I tell him, he disappears for a minute, bringing back the two batteries I need, big weighty black boxes. Twenty five pounds, a small price to pay to know we won't be without them.

Always something that needs sorting out, no different from having a house, the more you live in it the more you notice what needs doing. Two holes have appeared in the sunroof at the front of the van, I don't know when that happened, little holes open to the sky, they could easily let water in. Our sunroof's from a Land Rover and there's a Land Rover garage on the industrial estate too. The mechanic at the garage is helpful, says it's just a couple of screws we need, recommends a Land Rover breakers yard a few miles away. When we get there the yard is chaotic, full of smashed up, half disassembled Land Rovers and car parts. A cheery guy emerges from one of the wreckages, tousled hair, dirty overalls, tool belt loose around his waste and a wide gait of a walk, like a man who knows his shoelaces are undone. He takes a look at what we need, disappears inside one of the wreckages, brings us the screws, says to just give him a fiver.

Outside Exeter there's a restaurant that has music one night a week, it doesn't pay much but we get a pizza and a drink. Nobody is bothered about the music though, least of all the staff. They put us away from where customers are sitting like we're doing something antisocial. At the end when we get our money the waiter says to email the manager and they'll offer us another date. We'll probably take it.

Then to the small seaside fishing village of Polperro in Cornwall. A pub on the quayside. One big car park on the edge of town, the roads are narrow, not built for vehicles. A local says it's possible to park down on the harbour if we need to take the van in and unload. For some reason we listen to him. The street corner that leads into the harbour is so tight you can only turn into it from one direction so we drive past and up the hill, turn around and come back. It's so narrow, we put both wing mirrors in, they're millimetres away from the brickwork as the van edges slowly through. Smokers outside the pub see us arrive,

"They're all waiting for you."

For   some   reason   there's   been   a

miscommunication about when the start time is. We go in, there's a big cheer from the crowd that we've arrived. The pub is small, standing room only, wooden beams and low ceilings. Everyone is stood around us, on top of us as we hurriedly set up and kick off.

Half time and one of the guys stood right near us lifts his pint glass up, says hi, says his name's Simon but everyone calls him Ronnie, says he's having a great night. His house is next door, we should stop by and say hello sometime.

At the end of the night we drive off the harbour and have to go back through the narrow section of street again to get out. We got through it coming here but now it looks impossibly thin. As we edge forward the walls close in around us, it's definitely narrower this way. Both wing mirrors are in but along the bottom corner of the walls there are some small concrete wedges on both sides. We didn't notice them earlier.

Some of the locals on their way home from the pub start to offer drunken advice,

"I think I saw a van come through here once."

We reverse back out to line up better, slowly edging forward to try again, the locals offer more advice,

"There's a car park on the edge of town you could've used."

Reversing again, shifting our angle slightly, lining up for another go,

"Next time you could park there."

Then committing, slowly, a little revving to get over the concrete bumps, then slowly again, inch by inch.

How we make it I don't know, how we make it without scratching the van I've even less idea. We both shake our heads passing the car park on the way out of town.

Deeper into Cornwall to Porkellis, a tiny village not far from Helston. A pub that has music occasionally, when they do they make a big deal of it, the locals really like it. Whilst we're playing, one of them sends a message to a friend, a practical joke implying some famous musicians have stopped by and anyone not at the pub is missing out on something special. Like Chinese whispers the message spirals out of control. Residents of Porkellis and the local area who aren't at the pub start believing that Mumford and Sons have turned up to play an impromptu gig in town. So much so that the prank gets a write up and is featured in the local paper the following week. There's nothing we can use as a review or testimonial though.

We go back to Polperro. Maybe it was our lucky escape from the harbour, through the narrow street we barely got out of, maybe we just want to saunter into town, walk on foot through the tiny streets, unencumbered by a vehicle. Small painted houses looking out to sea, so close together, almost on top of one another. The quay is a working harbour full of old fishing boats, fishing nets, coils of rusty red and bottle green ropes around the edge of the dock.

We knock on the door next to the pub, the one we guess that Ronnie must live in. He answers,

"Great to see you, come in. This is the couple I was telling you about."

He introduces us to his wife and we sit with drinks looking out over the harbour,

"Where do you two live?"

We're still getting used to the question, Jayne and I exchange a brief look. We tell them, we've sold up, our VW is kind of our home now. They get it, they've got a VW van too and have done big trips across Europe in it, they think our back up plan of driving to the south of Spain in the winter is a good one. Maybe we'll never get used to the question about where we live because the response will always depend on who's asking it.

We try busking in Newquay. It's right out of season now, October, getting colder, the town just isn't busy. After making the effort to walk in with our gear we tell ourselves we've got to play, at least for a little while. Setting up on the only pedestrian street, people coming by now and then. I'm thinking what the hell are we doing here, I know Jayne's thinking the same. Neither of us dare say it, trying to keep up troop morale.

A cafe nearby has a couple of tables outside, just warm enough for customers to sit and have a drink. One couple sit there, sipping hot drinks but they never look at us. When they get up to leave they come over, thank us for the music and put a £5 note in the guitar case. You never can tell. That's about as good as it's going to get in Newquay, we put everything away and push the trolley back to the van.

Where else could we go? Padstow's not far, about fifteen miles up the coast. Maybe that'll be busier. It's cutting it fine, it'll be late afternoon by the time we get can there, get into town and set up.

By 3pm we're winding our way down into Padstow. The River Camel going in and out of view until the last hairpin bend brings us level with the town and the estuary. Quite a bit of traffic on the road, it must be a little busy.

We take the nearest car park to the centre, pay the premium rate and load up the trolley. Not much of the afternoon left, this isn't the time to hide down a side street so we set up on the quayside. Right in the middle, the sea and harbour behind us, the sound of seagulls overhead. Are we even allowed to do this? Play music right in the centre of Padstow? There's one way to find out.

People are strolling past with ice creams, eating fish and chips on benches. We start gently, easily, feeling our way into it. Passers by smile, give us a thumbs up or a thank you, money starts getting thrown in the case. The sun comes out, there's a sense of being in the right place at the right time. Three women come along, middle-aged ladies, happy, unselfconscious, they're in a festive mood, laughing and making excited noises, they ask,

"Where have you two come from?"

Not in a way that needs an answer, they dance together on the street to the music. Over to the left I see a police car pull into the main square, it slows to a stop, the policemen look over at us, at the ladies dancing, the people sat around on benches. Then they drive away through the square and out of view.

The sun stays out into the early evening, an echo of late summer, all warm and still, not even a breeze. The cold morning fifteen miles away in Newquay feels like a week ago or more. We're tired by the time we get back to the van but there's enough in the case when we count it up to book a Travelodge for tomorrow night.

Three o'clock in the afternoon is the earliest we can check in, we turn up at half two,

"I know we're early but..."

They're fine about it and we're in, luxuriating in the bath, watching trash TV, a picnic on the bed. I'm sure for most people the experience is functional, second or third best to being at home or anywhere else for that matter, something they can't wait to leave. For us it's our home for the night, all mod cons, we have running water, heating, a shower, electricity, a kettle, space around the bed to walk around barefoot. In the evening I can see out of our window into the car park, some of the businessmen and contractors sitting in cars and vans looking at their phones. Their front seat's more homely and familiar to them than a Travelodge room.

A few years ago on a holiday in Cornwall, we tried a Bed and Breakfast. We rang the doorbell, the owner answered, he brought us into the quiet hallway, the sound of a steady tick of a grandfather clock. He gave us the room key, then listed the items that would be included in the breakfast tomorrow,

"Eggs, tomatoes, beans..."

Quite a comprehensive list too, sounded good as he reeled off an extensive menu.

Next morning we went down to the breakfast room, the owner was busy serving guests, moving swiftly from table to table. He came over to ours, a little notebook and pencil in his hand, keeping his words brief,

"What can I get you?"

"Can you remind us what there is?"

He clenched the notebook and pencil,

"I told you yesterday."

There's no cooked breakfast at a Travelodge but there's a faceless anonymity that suits us fine.

The Barbican in Plymouth has a bar with music on a Friday night. They serve noodles, a kind of cabaret setting, a proper stage, lights and a soundman. Everyone's eating and talking while we play but we're fed with noodles and we get paid. Tables full of small groups, couples out on dates. Romantic couples are the best kind of audience, they talk quietly, whispering, looking for something special to make their night, something to remember.

Often after they've eaten they turn their chairs towards us, hold hands and listen.

On Saturday night we're in Looe. For a Cornish town it's easily accessible, on the flat, one road takes you in, round past the bars, shops and restaurants. We park outside to unload. The barmaid's wearing a Black Sabbath t-shirt, leaning back against the counter talking with some locals drinking at the bar. She looks over at us, we're standing with our instruments, she waits for us to speak.

"Hi, we're here to play music tonight."

She points over to the window, as we go to set up I hear someone say something, the locals at the bar laugh.

No complementary drink. Fortunately a group of students on a camping trip in some nearby woods come in to get warm, get drunk and party. They make loads of appreciative noise with everything we play, the barmaid begrudgingly hands over our money at the end of the night.

Over the bridge on the other side of town there's a huge car park, signs say no overnight sleeping but we tuck ourselves in between the cars at the busy end and take our chance. In the morning we drive to the quiet side overlooking the river, make coffee and hang out. I start an Instagram account, wildwoodjack, and put our first ever picture up, a photo of a small yellow boat moored on the river. Two seagulls sitting on it, one looking forward, the other back. The picture gets one like, from a guy called todd1.

A week from now we've got to be in Harrogate in Yorkshire. Jayne's mum was born nearby, there's a family get together to celebrate her 80th birthday. We'll try busking our way up.

One more gig in St. Ives then we start the long drive out of Cornwall, carrying on into the evening. It starts to rain heavily, lashing down onto the windscreen, so we pull into a motorway service area and pay to park for the night. At a covered picnic table under a fluorescent light I cook us a meal on the stove, the rain's making the weather feel colder. Then sitting in the front seat with our bowls of pasta, looking out at the wet picnic table, the stove and the frying pan. Will it be any different when we're in Italy? I hope the weather there holds out for awhile.

The next day we carry on up the motorway, the weather's still not sure what it's doing. It starts to clear up as we get near Cheltenham so we drive in, decide to try playing there. In town there's no competition on the main street and we set up and play between two shop entrances.

A young guy in a tracksuit and baseball cap comes up, he's with his girlfriend, she's shy, standing further away. He asks if we'll announce before the next song that Daz loves Bridey B. Sure we will, Jayne clears her throat as if she's making an important announcement, says over the microphone,

"I want to say that Daz loves Bridey B."

The young couple stand together a few feet away as we play the next song, he's got his arm around her, he's grinning, she's looking down, nudging him, blushing. Afterwards they come over, he's pleased with how it went, he looks in our guitar case,

"I'd give you some money but you've got more than me."

We try Sheffield, it's full of buskers. On the main pedestrian street, there's a dance troupe, charity collections, energy switching companies and a guy playing saxophone at a loud volume to a backing track. Further up the street I see a classical guitarist. After he's finished playing a piece I ask him how long he'll be there,

"All day."

Jayne asks a shopper where else someone might play in town. They say they've seen musicians on the road that leads to the university, it's not far, just round the corner, much quieter, more easy going. We pick up the lunchtime footfall, students and lecturers going back and forth for coffee and sandwiches.

Doncaster's busy too. The best pitch is taken by two South American guys playing pan pipes to a backing track, all through a P.A. powered by a generator. There's a third guy with them selling CD's, merchandise, dream catchers, we ask him how long they're going to be there,

"All day."

We find somewhere else. A lady comes up, says she's the person responsible for busking in the town centre, says we need permission, they'll give us a permit when we make an official application. Says we can carry on today though.

Then Harrogate for Jayne's mum's 80th birthday celebrations, there's a big meal at the hotel where family are staying, the hotel let us park and sleep in their car park. Poems and tributes are read out, we sing a couple of Beatles songs. Next day we go to Betty's Tea Room for afternoon tea and cake.

From now on the only direction we're going is south. Cold days are outnumbering warm ones. Autumn's really here, everywhere the leaves on the trees are turning shades of red and gold, just a few days and a couple of gigs before the clocks go back and we cross the channel.

On the way south we go busking in Huntingdon. As we're playing, a blind lady walks slowly up the street, feeling her way with her white stick. She comes level with us, stops, then gently waves her walking stick in our direction, tapping the side of the guitar case lying open in front of us. At the end of the song she says,

"Are you playing that music?"

"Yes we are."

She reaches into her handbag, takes her purse out, drops some coins in the case and carries on.

Another guy comes up to say hi. He and his wife had been planning to move to Ireland but she died recently. William, not long retired, he's sold the house and is still going, nervous about the prospect of moving somewhere new on his own. Tears fill up in his eyes as he talks about his plans. William loves country music, writes and records his own songs. He gives us his email address and says we're welcome to go and stay anytime if ever we make it over to Ireland.

Our last gig's in Peterborough, on a bar on a boat, afterwards we pack up quickly to get on the next boat, the ferry. Then a drive straight down through France, hoping to get ahead of the weather, chase the sunshine but it's cold and rains for most of the way. The side window at the back has started leaking, inside round the top edge is wet. I dry it off on the outside and put gaffer tape over it, it seems to do the trick, have to get that sorted at some point.

6. DO YOU WANT TO DANCE?

J ayne has a good friend Joni, her and her partner have a chalet in the mountains in France, not far from the Italian border. We haven't seen them for years, haven't had the chance, Jayne's excited, wants to drive straight there. The plan'll be to spend a couple of nights with them then head straight for Lucca, the Comics and Games Festival. Then who knows? Busk around Italy for as long as the weather holds out, the south of Spain after? Jayne's joined a house sitting site, something might happen with that.

To get to Joni's village, Valfréjus, you have to drive to the entrance of the Mont Blanc Tunnel, the one that takes you through the Alps from France into Italy. That's what the satnav says. It's evening by the time we're climbing up the road to Mont Blanc, the closer we get the more tunnel signs there are, big serious signs, toll and warning signs, are we sure this is the right way to Valfréjus? Doesn't look like there's any way back now. The satnav definitely says this is the way, go to the entrance of the tunnel and turn around. Now isn't the time for us to start talking about what the satnav says you can and can't do, things never turn out well with that conversation.

More toll signs, then up ahead, the mouth of the tunnel, a tunnel over seven miles long, we don't want to find ourselves driving through that, paying the tolls twice because we'd have to come back again. Just as we approach, almost to the tunnel, there's a small road sign, a little arrow showing a U-turn for Valfréjus. A sigh of relief. We message Joni, we're nearly there. She messages straight back, drive on up, you'll find us, we're the ones in the village drinking wine on a balcony.

Valfréjus is a ski resort but there's no snow right now, most of the chalets are unoccupied. Easy to spot the one with drinkers on the balcony, waving, cheering at us, silhouetted by the warm light coming from their living room. Our arrival's treated as a celebration, they fill Jayne's glass to the brim, she deserves it, driving through the whole of France in a day. Joni's always effervescent and charming, very well spoken too, calls her partner Broo. He's Australian, Bruce, but I don't think she's ever called him that. She's made a hearty meal for the four of us, stocked up the kitchen with supplies from the shops at the base of the mountain.

We sit round the hot glow of the log burner, they're here for the winter, the snow's coming soon. Broo loves to ski, he works in IT and can work anywhere. Their plan is to renovate a boat they've recently bought in Turkey and spend the summer on that, mooring up at harbours for wi-fi when they need it.

Next day we take a walk through the village and the mountain paths around it, past the unoccupied chalets, the stationary chair lifts. All waiting for the snow to arrive. It's so quiet our footsteps echo back from the chalet walls. Snow's arriving soon, probably in the next two weeks, by then you'll need snow chains on your car tyres to drive up here. We talk about the next leg of our journey, Italy just over the Alps, the most direct route through the Mont Blanc Tunnel. Bruce says it's expensive, especially with a van, recommends the mountain road, the scenic route if we're not in a hurry, just a couple of extra hours on the journey. Right now it's clear, the snow's late, it'll be impassable once it's arrived, blocked off for the whole of winter.

When we say goodbye, none of us can say when we'll see each other again. At the bottom of the mountain we pick up baguettes from the local store, then we're winding up and up again, through the Alps to the French border. A clear day, the sun is out, the views extend for miles. Nobody seems to use this road, we barely see another car, just mountains as far as the eye can see, pine trees and patches of snow sprinkled across the landscape. At the top the road levels out and we stop for lunch, break open the baguettes and make coffee, soon we'll be drinking Italian coffee.

As we cross the border and start the descent into Italy the road follows the contours of the mountains again, an endless S-shape through steep evergreen forests. Then around Turin and we head down to the coast. About another two hundred and fifty miles to Lucca, all of it motorway. The service stations, Autogrills, every twenty kilometres or so, we're spoilt for choice about where to stop for coffee, we let the first few pass by then pull into one.

The first thing you have to know is that you can't just walk up to the counter where the barristas are to get your coffee. No, you have to go to a separate cash desk, order from the cashier who gives you a receipt that you take to the barrista. There's usually a big huddle of people along the counter, well dressed Italians drinking from little cups, it can take time to get noticed,

"*Due machiatti.*"

The barrista nods in a way that says we've made a good choice, strikes his fingernail across the receipt. Then his arms make a short, precise sequence of movements before two little cups and saucers are placed gently in front of us. Making coffee in Italy is a career choice, not just a temporary job whilst you're a student. Not served in some huge cup either, like more is somehow better. It's a small pleasure to be appreciated, savoured and enjoyed, we clink our little cups together as a way of saying we've landed.

Then back on the road, maybe we'll stop again before too long. Beautiful bright sunlight greets us on the highway along the Ligurian Sea, disappearing and reappearing as we go in and out of the tunnels that cut through the hills. Then around Genoa, staying on the coast, Lucca just a hundred miles away.

When we get to Lucca we circle around the outside of the city walls, there's a big car park the festival have taken over, guys with money belts selling parking tickets wave us into a space. Six euros and we can stay overnight, it looks like others are doing the same. It's going to be busy, the biggest comic festival in Europe, around two hundred thousand people are supposed to be coming in.

Next morning we're loaded up, wheeling the trolley into the centre. A lot of people dressed as their favourite character, characters from comics, films, computer games, novels. Cosplay, anyone dressed in a costume is up for saying hi. We exchange *buongiornos* and *ciaos* with a Super Mario, some Storm Troopers, Batman, Spiderman and a host of other's we don't even recognise. Before we're even near the centre Jayne says,

"What about here?"

A pedestrian street, plenty of people making their way in and out of town. Why not? We set up, start to play, a crowd gather, quite a big crowd, a proper audience. Italians smiling, happy and clapping at this impromptu concert. Everyone's in a good mood. We play a short set, the street's residential, we decide that's enough, quit while we're ahead. Jayne announces our final number, it has the right effect, there's the final applause, people step forward and drop coins in the case. That was alright, looking at the money, I reckon there's more than sixty euros in there.

Our old piazza, the one with the statue of Giacomo Puccini, is way too busy and noisy. Likewise the main square in the centre is too, people shoulder to shoulder, so much distraction, more costumes here than anywhere else in town. It's like a movie studio between takes, multiple characters, multiple films, all being made at the same time.

There are smaller walkways leading into the main square, on one of them we walk by a busker, a young guy in green tights and a tunic playing a little harp, dressed as Zelda from the Nintendo computer game. We move further up the street from him, go opposite a corner cafe. When we start to play a young waitress darts out of the cafe through the crowd, puts a five euro note in our case. People seem to like the music, coins get dropped as the city bustles past, a constant stream of cartoon characters, costumes, locals and tourists. It feels like we've made a good choice, coming to Lucca at the start of winter.

The next day we head straight back in and set up opposite the cafe. Just like yesterday, as soon as we start playing the waitress comes over with a five euro note. It's busy again, maybe more so, the little street full of fantasy characters mixed with everyday folk. Ten minutes in and two men appear in front of us in policeman's costumes. Wait a

minute! They're not in costume, they are policemen,
"Stop, come with us."

This one's short, round faced with a big
moustache, large waistline, a well polished leather
belt. His sidekick is much thinner, standing behind
his shoulder, both have serious looks on their faces.
They also have the harp guy in the green leotard
with them as well. We pack up our trolley and go
with them through the busy streets, a few blocks to
the police station. Have we just been arrested? The
harp guy's from Poland, he can speak a bit of English,
he doesn't know either. The same thing happened to
him while he was playing, the police told him to stop
and come with them.

At the police station we're taken into an
office, desks with computers on them. We're told to
sit on chairs in the corner of the room. Two other
plain clothes police come in, there's a conversation
between them all, they're all standing up, one of
them leans over a computer terminal, taps some
keys, moves the mouse. Then they all leave. Jayne
speaks Italian but she's not sure what's going on.
The Polish guy speaks some Italian too but he also
doesn't know what's going on. Well, we're not in a
police cell, we have no handcuffs on. The Polish guy
is young, in his early twenties, blonde, slightly built,
effeminate but maybe that's just the green tights
and tunic. We talk about busking, he says he's been
in Pisa, there's one street you're allowed to busk on
there and he tells us where it is, the rest of it is out of
bounds though. He did okay.

The policemen come back in, huddle around another computer, taking it in turns to tap some keys or point somewhere on the screen. They seem to be looking for something. Another officer comes in to help, there's a lot of dialogue, a lot of leaving and entering the room. The policeman that picked us up looks like the larger member of Laurel and Hardy, he's doing most of the work, most of the sweating anyway, he's the one that's got to sort out whatever's going on. At one point he comes over, breathes out a couple of times and points, first at us and then at the Polish guy,

"You, good persons, okay."

Then he leaves the room again. What did he mean by that? Is he letting us off or sorry for what he's about to do?

More comings and goings, then a new guy, he knows something none of the others do, with a few taps on the keyboard he finds what they're looking for. Our man sits down in front of the screen, a minute later he stands up in a brisk accomplished fashion. We hear the whir of the printer, the sound of documents chugging they're way out of the machine. A lot of documents. They're stacked together, shuffled into two piles and squared off loudly on the table top. There's one for us and one for the Polish guy.

With some careful reading and attempts at translation it turns out we have to sign it and agree to it's terms. There's only one spot in town that buskers are allowed to play, on the steps in the main square. No other performances are allowed anywhere else in town, if we're caught violating this at any point in the future we'll have to pay a fine of fifty euros. We all sign it and are free to go.

Outside the Police Station we say goodbye and good luck to our Polish friend. He's not sure what he's going to do now, maybe go to Pisa again. As we make our way back through the main square we pass the spot, the one spot where you're actually allowed to play. It's so crowded and chaotic, it'd be impossible, maybe even dangerous to try and play here during the festival. Seems we just got lucky in the summer, back in August we somehow got away with it. So we go back to the van, put our stuff away and do what any Italian would do under the circumstances. Go back into town and eat pizza.

I message our friend Paulo, the one man band and full time busker from Rimini. He gives me some suggestions of where we could go, puts me in touch with his friend Fabrizio who busks too. I message him, he comes back with places we could try. Fabrizio has just come back from Spain, he says the Spanish love street music but didn't put much in his hat.

The obvious place to go is Pisa, it's only half an hour away, maybe we'll bump into our Polish friend. He said you can busk anywhere up the first part of Corso Italia, the street that leads from the statue near the railway station into town. The historic centre of Pisa is totally out of bounds, you're not allowed to play anywhere there.

Corso Italia's a nice wide pedestrian street, busy enough as it's the main route from the station into the centre. The first part looks okay but the next block looks better. We'll just plead ignorance and politeness if we've gone too far up, we can always say we didn't know, we're still this side of the river, a long way from the historic centre.

The street runs past a tiny piazza, a little cafe on it's corner. There's a gold statue in the middle in front of a terracotta coloured church, the cafe has outdoor seating, there's even a bench for passers by. The whole scene feels good. We set up in front of the statue facing the street. The owner of the cafe offers us coffee, puts money in our case and buys a CD.

We return again in the late afternoon, when we arrive the coffee bar is playing our CD on their stereo, the barman waves to us. Later on a police car drives by slowly, the policemen look at us as they drive by but carry on, I'm not sure but I think one of them was shaking his head.

After Pisa we just pick the next city. Livorno looks worth trying, only half an hour away, a big population, over 150,000. Even in the week it should be busy. We drive around endlessly looking for somewhere unrestricted to park, end up around two kilometres away from the centre. It takes ages to walk in, we have no idea where to go, we're hoping to find some sort of central pedestrian area. There are some beautiful colonnades with fancy shops and banks but they're on streets with traffic. We find a short walkway full of market traders conducting important business, Italian ladies earnestly buying groceries, it doesn't feel right. We're running out of time, it's midday now, the shops shut in an hour. Away from the centre we come across a road with barriers at either end, the street blocked from traffic, pedestrianised when the shops are open. If this isn't going to be a wasted trip we've got to give it a go. With 30 minutes left before everything shuts for lunch we play our best songs and get a good response from the last of the shoppers. Three hours now to wait until they open again at 4pm, no point going back to the van, it's too far.

There's a park nearby, we eat a picnic, lie out in the sunshine. Lucky with the weather at the moment, it's November, when the sun shines it's warm. We get sleepy but don't feel like sleeping. Coffee will wake us up, there's a cafe in the piazza a stones throw from our busking street. It's clearly a locals bar, people taking their time over drinks, no ones in a hurry, it's the afternoon. The tables are close together, there's a free one by the window, a well dressed, dark haired, good looking couple are sat near it, they look over, smile, we all say hi. They remark on the instruments on our trolley then discover we're English, we get talking, their names are Robert and Roberta. They're both in suits, dressed for business, this is Italy though, it could be what they wear on a day off.

I once heard about a traveller who was asked what it was like continuously meeting strangers, meeting so many people for the first time. He said for him it was all about whether they want to dance, about whether people want to engage with you freely in the moment and enjoy it for what it is.

Robert and Roberta want to dance. We start talking, they're here on business, live further down the coast, say there's a lot of sunshine for November, unusual for this time of year. We talk through the afternoon about everything and anything, about the sunshine, about whether they'll get married, food, business and life until we realise it's time for us to go, the shops are about to open again.

Then we head towards Perugia, Paulo, our one man band friend has recommended the city. We decide to stop on the way, take a break, a road sign says the next town's Arezzo. Pulling into the south of the city, we park up, take a walk round town. The pedestrian streets are perfect for playing but there's no one around. A restaurant is open, empty tables outside, a waiter idly standing by the front door,

"Does anyone play music on the streets here?"

He says they do, but this time of year it's only busy on Fridays and Saturdays. Wednesday today, we decide to wait, hang out until the start of the weekend. The city's built on a big hill, the suburbs are on the flat plains below it. Round to the north is a car park for camper vans We follow the ring road until we're the other side of the city, passing by a small row of shops, turning into a residential area, past apartment blocks, then down a long straight quiet street. The street runs alongside a football pitch, at the far end is the official camper van car park. A small, square piece of new tarmac, like it's just been built, a new ticket machine and a tariff sign, there's no one parked on it, it's empty. There are a couple of motor homes parked on the opposite side of the street though, they look dusty, weathered, forgotten, left here for the winter, or maybe forever. No one's in them but there's space to park next to them, perpendicular, facing the road, facing the football pitch.

The drive from the other side of town has disorientated us, we've turned corners so many times it's not clear how to get from here into the centre. An elderly lady in a pink cardigan comes past walking her little dog, a small brown terrier in a red and white checked jacket. Jayne asks the woman for directions and they get talking, her name is Bruna, she lives just the other side of the football pitch. A little over five foot tall with a boyish face, dark rimmed spectacles, short brown hair, only a wisp or two of grey. Her little dog is called Lola, Jayne makes a fuss of Lola as she explains to Bruna that we're musicians, waiting for the weekend, waiting to play music on the streets in town. Bruna gestures with her hands explaining the way in, she says "Scale Mobili" a few times. When she's gone I ask Jayne what she meant,

"I think she said to take the escalator."

So we walk in, back up past the football pitch, the apartment blocks, cross the ring road then through smaller streets, signs for the Scale Mobili. They point us to the bottom of a steep hill, so steep this way into town that they've built an escalator. It's under cover and takes us up in three stages, the inside wall has a huge mural running the full length of it, giant heads of men in a medieval battle. Some in suits of armour, others in hats and helmets, intense determined faces looking up and down the moving staircase as we ride up. Lances, spears and swords criss-cross the wall, the eyes and ears of horses just in view. A battle to reclaim the original wood from Christ's cross, stolen from Jerusalem by a Persian king. The recreation of a painting by Piero della Francesca, resident of Arezzo.

I know this because the escalator delivers us to a courtyard with a tourist office and gift shop. I'm browsing the information while Jayne uses the loo. Another famous son of the city is Guido of Arezzo, a Benedictine monk who invented musical notation in the eleventh century. From the tourist office there's one final shorter escalator then a passageway through a historic building and we're standing by a massive cathedral at the top of the city. What a city it is! Ancient, grand, like Lucca, I can't believe it's not on the main tourist trails. Maybe it is. Then again, this is Italy, home of over half of all the World Heritage Sites.

From the huge cathedral, at the top of the hill, a choice of pedestrian arteries lead you down the other side. The one furthest left takes you past Piazza Grande, a beautiful square, built on a slope. At the bottom corner of the piazza is a tenth century church with a vaulted entrance, next to this a palace with a semi circular stairway leading up to its front doors. So much history crammed into one space. Reminders around town that this square and other parts of Arezzo were used in the Roberto Benigni film *Life is Beautiful*.

We rejoin the main walkway, the number of shops and cafes increase as we make our way down, this is where we'll play. The only thing about that is the effort that'll be needed to get the trolley here and back again when we come in on Friday.

So we're waiting for the weekend. On Thursday we shop at the little row of stores nearby. I open up the tailgate of the van, put our table up and cook a meal, mushroom risotto. Bruna and her dog Lola walk by and she stops to chat. She can see I'm cooking, is interested to know what I'm making. Jayne tells her I'm making risotto, she says it proudly, like it'll impress a local, an Englishman making Italian food. Bruna comes over to the stove, peers into the pan, lifting her chin while her eyes roll down, takes a little sniff. She shakes her head slowly like there's bad news to deliver, Lola's pulling on the lead eager to carry on walking.

Early evening after dark, the quiet road suddenly fills with parked cars, floodlights of the football pitch come on. Young guys with big sports bags arrive, slamming doors, hurrying into the changing rooms. The air is wet and cold. We sit in the front seat facing the pitch, see them emerge from the small building in their kit, kicking their legs out, jumping up and down, stretching, bantering with each other until the match starts. The game's punctuated by the referees whistle, the shouts of the players, the cheers of a few spectators who've come to watch.

The final whistle pierces the night, echoes round the neighbourhood and they all file into the changing room and back out again with their kit bags. Car doors slam, one after another after another. Engines starting, they pull away, their tail lights disappearing until there's just us and a quiet street again.

Friday morning, Bruna and Lola come by. She's brought us a present, a brown paper bag full of foraged mushrooms. The bag smells of the earthy dampness of a forest floor. Her son and his dog have been out in the woods and picked them, fungi, big, dark brown and cream coloured, meaty and pungent. Strict instructions on how to use them too, how to make proper risotto. Bruna gestures with her arms and hands, takes out a mushroom, holding it delicately between her fingers, talking, intense, serious. I nod out of politeness but can't follow what she's saying, Jayne's making positive noises, she must know what she wants us to do.

Then we load up the trolley for the trip into town, the morning session. The escalator has warning signs about heavy luggage so I have to push it up the long steep hill. Leaning right into it, all my body weight behind it, taking a section at a time, pausing, then gearing up for another run. It's a workout and we stop at the top for me to steady myself and catch my breath. Then back down the other side, a different set of muscles this time, balancing the trolley to stop it running away from me.

About halfway down the pedestrian alley that leads to the centre of town, where the steepness flattens to a more gentle slope, there's a small modern cafe bar. An open glass door, black signage above it, a logo of a trilby hat sitting on the white letters of it's name, 'My Way'. It's empty inside, a couple of tables outside, the owner is standing in the doorway, smiles when he sees our instruments and gear. We say hi, Jayne asks if we can set up opposite. He likes the idea, so we play on the other side of the walkway facing back towards the cafe. It's not so busy on the street but a few passers by stop and have coffee at the tables then drop euros in the case when they leave. The owner says there'll be more people around tonight. I ask if we can leave our equipment somewhere safe until later, save pushing it back up the hill and down the other side. No problem he says, pointing to the back of the cafe. Inside it's still empty and quiet, I wonder if he ever gets busy. There's a back room with a sink and some metal shelves, I leave it next to a mop and bucket in the corner and close the door. We go back to the van for lunch, to our brown paper bag of foraged mushrooms. Jayne thinks she's remembered the instructions about how to cook them, but if Bruna comes by she might have a different opinion.

The owner of the bar is right, the town is busier later. Friday night, more Italians are coming out to enjoy the evening, even when the shops shut, they're strolling around the city, arm in arm, hand in hand, the tradition of a parade around town. La Passagiata, a well-dressed evening walk, no destination, no hurry. Maybe they'll walk past two English musicians playing in town, maybe they'll like the sound the musicians are making and they'll stop for awhile. It might put a smile on their face, lift their spirits a little, maybe a hand goes in a pocket, comes out with a coin to drop.

Numbers increase until the street becomes too noisy and we feel out of place, we've been going for hours, by now the feeling that our time is up can't be ignored. We scoop the coins into our money bag, there's a good weight to it, some euro notes too.

Underneath the buzz of it all I can feel that heavy feeling, the energy disappearing, hunger, tiredness creeping in.

We search around the back streets nearby for something to eat, something cheap, easy, not too far away. Teenagers are gathered outside a Turkish takeaway, one of them casually sat on the back of a moped. Inside there are more teenagers, grouped around the counter, we wheel the trolley in, stand behind them. Their voices are excited, all talking at once, pausing in turn to order the same thing, flatbreads with salad and falafel, topped with French fries, a big squeeze of mayonnaise and ketchup. They move aside and sit at one of the plastic tables. We want what they've got, order two, take them to a free table. Their evening sounds like it's just starting, like they're getting ready to go somewhere. Civilised though, sipping from bottles of water and fizzy drinks, talking, eating. I go and fetch more napkins, our fingers are covered in mayonnaise and ketchup, running down our hands and onto the table.

The salt, fat and fizzy drink energy is what we need to get us home, get us back up the hill. We roll the trolley past the 'My Way' bar where the slope gets steeper, it's real identity is now revealed. Italian kids spilling out of it's front doors, bright lights flashing inside, music pumping onto the street. No chance of leaving our gear here this time, we push on up, we'll be back to do it all again tomorrow.

After the weekend we leave Arezzo. Bruna came to see us before we left and gave us her address, said to come and say hello if we're ever passing, we gave her one of our CD's. Jayne picked up Lola and gave her extra fuss as we said goodbye.

We head south and carry on with the intention of going busking in Perugia. When we get there it's raining, cold and overcast. On the outskirts there's a launderette, a *lavanderia*, on a corner next to a row of shops, we decide to do our washing instead.

With busking you never need to think about having change, supermarket cashiers only have so much patience when it comes to counting out money but a machine will wait for ages while you feed it coins. This *lavanderia* has a central terminal that controls everything, you tell it which number your washing's in, no need for powder or conditioner, it does it all. We sort out the smallest coins, the one's that are hardest to get rid of elsewhere, then push them into the slot next to the computerised console. No one else is in here, just a couple of machines gently whirring away next to each other. It feels good putting all the dirty clothes in, watching the machine click into action, start filling with soap and water. It starts to hum and slowly spin, the display says it'll take 40 minutes, enough time for coffee and pastry at the cafe next door.

Rain is giving the air a cold bite, feels like we're moving through to the end of autumn. The cafe next door is warm, hot air from a heater over the door, a few older guys having morning cappuccinos, reading the paper. There's a television up on the wall tuned to a music video channel that no one's watching.

I order two coffees and two croissants, make it clear we want the plain ones, *vuoto*, empty, that's how they describe them. Sometimes they say *senza niente*, without nothing, it varies from region to region.

The bar has high chairs at the front window where we can watch the passers by, the rain splashing down making puddles on the pavement. Umbrellas, Italian men in their winter wardrobe, thick woollen coats, scarves tied in stylish knots around their necks as a statement piece, like a ribbon and bow finishing the wrapping of a gift.

My eye gets drawn back inside to the television screen, another music video. A young good looking guy, singing to camera, on a yacht, then on a jet ski. Then he's alone in a villa on the side of a mountain. The music's turned down low, I can only just make out some of the lyrics, I think he's missing someone.

When we get back to the launderette there's a man pacing up and down on his mobile phone. He looks over expectantly as we go in, lowering the phone from his face, then disappointment when he sees us and he lifts it back to his ear and carries on pacing up and down. He hangs up. His washing's stuck in one of the dryers and he can't get it out, a problem with the lock not releasing. There's an emergency number, he keeps ringing it but no one's answering. We go over to our machine, it's finished it's cycle, the washing sat in a stationary heap inside. Tentatively Jayne presses the button, there's a solid click and the door swings open. The guy tries his dryer door again, no luck. She drags the tangled wet clothes out and into a basket, the guy's getting more frustrated, why isn't his door opening? He tries the phone number again, no answer.

What should we do? Should we risk putting our clothes in a dryer? I don't think so, wet washing in the hand is worth two loads stuck in a machine. Too risky, we'll need to find another launderette. It's still raining outside and the forecast doesn't look good for busking, says it'll rain all day, in fact, rain for the next few days. The clouds are all black on the weather map, everywhere round this area, but they disappear further north where they turn to little white ones, a hopeful sun peeping out from behind. Quite a bit further north though, up near Bologna, three and a half hours away. What shall we do? Trust the forecast and go there? It's a place we know, Jayne and I spent some months there years ago as part of her university degree. We know a launderette too and can get this load dry.

So with a big pile of wet washing on our bed in the back of the van we set off for Bologna. Still raining, cold and damp outside, inside it's damp too, the soggy collection of clothes giving off a lot of condensation. Tonight we'll want to sleep in here. Possibly the first people to ever wash their clothes in Perugia and then drive to Bologna to dry them. Who knows, maybe there've been other mad laundry dogs or Englishmen that have done the same thing. With the pulse of the windscreen wipers clearing the rain away my mind wanders. Our behaviour would confound a surveillance team, random, unpredictable, the crackle of a walkie talkie,

"Where the hell are they going now?"

"They're travelling north again, it looks urgent."

"Eyes on the target?"

"Negative, the windows are steamed up."

By the time we get to Bologna it's starting to get dark. What with the road being busy, stopping for sandwiches, coffee and then fuel.

The launderette we use to use when Jayne studied here twenty years ago doesn't exist any more but there's another one not far away. Full of students, looking at their phones, flicking through magazines, every dryer's busy, everyone looking like they'd rather be somewhere else.

Eventually one becomes free and we unburden the cold, wet load into the machine, feed it a handful of coins. Watch as our clothes spin round, dancing happy cartwheels in the drum and tumbling their way to warmth. I've never sat in front of a drying cycle with such pleasure.

We know we can busk in Bologna, it's busy every day. Twenty years ago when Jayne was studying here we came out once and played on the street, not for long, I remember a priest coming by on a bicycle and dropping a coin in our case.

When it comes to busking, any spot that's worked out okay you always go back to first. Creatures of habit, which is why we head to where we went all those years ago, past Piazza Maggiore, the big central square in town, huge, grand and imposing. Down the pedestrian street that leads off from it's south west corner, a long strip of nice looking expensive shops on a walkway about twenty feet wide. Further up where the street narrows, you come to a red brick church on the right. The church has a side wall, the perfect place to play to passers by, not obscuring any shop windows.

Early evening, little audiences congregate, stop for awhile, listen to a few songs then put some coins in the case and move on. Once one person stops others soon join them. Like an empty dance floor, the first person to step onto it says yes, there's something worthwhile happening here, and everyone else follows.

We start to hear music coming from somewhere above us. There's a different atmosphere in the street, a woman puts her finger to her lips telling us to be quiet, a few more people stop, look up and listen. Following their gaze upward, I can see it, where the music's coming from, a balcony covered in plant pots and flower pots. Some of the crowd know the words to the song that's floating down from the speakers.

When the song stops an Italian guy explains it's where the singer and songwriter Lucio Dalla lived. He puts his hand on his chest, says that Dalla holds a special place in the hearts of the Italian people. That Dalla died in 2012, every evening since then they play a recording of one of his songs. He takes a photo of the balcony, says we've picked a good place to play under and it's okay to carry on now. We start playing again and a priest comes by on a bike, slows down and drops a coin in the case. I wonder if it's the same one as all those years ago, I like to think it is.

Bologna's on a motorway that cuts diagonally across the top half of Italy, an almost straight line 270 miles long. North west to Modena, Parma, then up to Piacenza and Milan. South east to Imola, Forli and Rimini where it runs along the coast to Ancona. Paulo, our busking friend has given us a heads up on some of the places we can go and some we can't, like Parma, he says the police will move you on. In some it'll depend on the day.

Imola is to the south, the next big town along from Bologna just 20 miles down the road. It's busy enough in a small piazza near two coffee bars and a bus stop. We get brave and stand right in the middle of the piazza. Strange looks from locals at the start, they're not sure what to make of us but we hold our nerve and eventually one of them breaks ranks and comes over to put a coin in the case, then others follow suit.

In the early evening we come back into town again but it's really quiet, there's no one around. There's a chill in the air and a wind coming down the main street. What to do, one of us always has to say,

"Well we're here, what else are we going to do?"

I think it's the quietest street we've ever played on, you can hear the footsteps of the next person coming. Plenty of time to reflect, to think, what are we doing here? Why are we doing this? It's getting cold now. With no home to go to, are we homeless standing here on the street, are we begging? We're no longer living in the spaces in between but have fallen through the cracks and disappeared. I try to put the thoughts out of my mind, remind myself the Italians call us 'Artisti della Strada', artists of the street. We're not far from a bar, the waitress takes pity on us and comes out and offers us a drink.

Imola should be much busier at the weekend. On Saturday morning the town is full. There's a good feeling about it and we take up a spot with a flow of people going past. A lady comes over and says there's a busking festival in Imola every year, we should apply, our music would be just right. Whilst we're talking a friendly policeman comes over and joins in the conversation too. He agrees about us being right for the street festival, then he says,

"You can't play now, it's not allowed outside of the festival."

He's very congenial, probably the nicest policeman to tell us to stop playing we've had but it's frustrating to have to pack our things up when the opportunity seems so good.

We drive up to Modena, it's foggy and we walk in alongside people wrapped in coats and scarves. There's a Piazza Grande here too, this one with a colonnade around part of it's edge so we play in the shelter beneath it. Quiet again, a man and woman walk by in a hurry but stop to listen when they see us, he's Italian but when he realises we're English he changes language and says to her,

"This is good music."

He's Gerardo and says he owns a pizzeria nearby,

"I'll make you pizza, come to my place."

We say we'll be there once we've finished. Just before 1pm, with all the shops about to close for lunch, a small crowd gathers around us for our last song. When we stop, one of them wants to buy a CD, that sets everyone off and they all want to buy one. The only thing is, we have five CD's in our case and there's seven of them. We've not restocked, with lower numbers of passers by, winter on the way, we've got lapse, we've not sold this many in one go for ages, probably never. Jayne keeps them in conversation and I run to the van. It takes about 15 minutes to get back again and they're all still talking.

We go to Gerardo's for pizza,

"Come in, come in."

He greets us like old friends, puts us at a table by the window,

"What would you like?"

Then he jumps behind the counter, energetic in his white apron, red t-shirt and black trousers, the classic uniform of a *pizzaiola*. He returns with freshly made pizza then grabs a guitar from somewhere out the back. Standing with one foot on a chair, the guitar resting on his knee he sings us a song. Jayne and I sit eating pizza, serenaded by a *pizzaiola*, this is why we came on the road.

So we get into a rhythm of where we're allowed to go, which towns and streets work best. Splitting the money we make three ways, the 2 euro coins are set aside for fuel, euro notes go in the winter envelope for later and the other coins cover food, drink and everything else. Most nights we drive onto the autostrade to a motorway services and spend the night there. That way we don't need to decide where to park up for the night, it's safe, easy and we can use the facilities. A short trip on the autostrade only costs a couple of euros, sometimes less. The next day the machine at the toll booth says we've taken too long to complete such a short journey. We feed it the money and it lets us through anyway, I suppose what else is it going to do?

Coming off the motorway one day we get a puncture and have to pull over as the road joins an intersection. I ring the European breakdown service and an hour later a guy in a big flatbed truck turns up. He's not interested in using the spare wheel, changing the tyre, he just wants to put us on the back of his flatbed and take us to his friend nearby, a tyre guy, a *gommista*.

The *gommista* says he can put a new tyre on for us, Jayne asks how much and he says,

"Do you need a receipt?"

"Is there a difference?"

He knocks twenty euros off the price and changes the wheel.

7. OLD CROWS AND SHADOWS

One night at the motorway services I'm making pasta on the stove outside while Jayne sits in the back of the van and does emails. Too cold now to leave the side door open, my breath mixes with the vapours rising off the boiling water as I'm stirring the pan. When I open the door to get back in she says,

"Guess what?"

The steam's rising off our bowls as I hand hers over, a one pot meal, spaghetti with ready made pesto,

"An English family want us to house sit in southern France."

Jayne's been checking a website every day for weeks, nothing's come up that's been practical to apply for. We don't have any testimonials either but this family have been let down at the last minute and are desperate. They live in a small town halfway between Narbonne and Carcassone, they need us next week.

I close my eyes for a second, I can't believe

it, imagine that? A house, hot water, electricity, a kitchen, a washing machine. We'll be surrounded by these luxuries, available at a moments notice. Not only that but the house sit is for eighteen days. Eighteen whole days, how about that? All we've got to do is look after their dog Ralph.

High on the thought of some downtime we look at the next week. We need to allow travel time, it's five hundred miles away, perhaps another farewell busk in Pisa and Livorno first, then start the journey, follow the coast up. Maybe stop somewhere on the way before the highway takes us out of Italy and into the south of France, like migrating birds on a flyway, following the trail.

So a farewell visit to Pisa first, but this time a policeman stops us playing in our favourite little piazza. He points down the street, says what the city rule is, where we can play, it's not here. With the palm of his hand open and his arm outstretched showing us the way, it's like he's saying it's time to go, time to leave. However, there's an early Christmas market and it does us a favour. Some of the traders are friendly and like us playing, the music's keeping their spirits up, encouraging passers by to stop longer and browse the stalls. It's working well for awhile and then it starts raining, really raining. We back into a shop doorway and take cover, the traders put waterproof ponchos on, close up the front of their stalls. Shoppers disappear until there's no one out on the street, the weather doesn't look like it's going to change. We pack up, go back to the van and put everything away.

"We haven't seen the leaning tower."

Jayne's right, we've never seen the main attraction. We've too much energy to sit in the van and watch droplets of rain trickle down the windscreen. It isn't going to let up either so we put all our waterproofs on and go out, walking back past our regular spot and up to the River Arno. The drizzle and mist in the air makes our jackets shiny, water drips off our hoods. Hardly anyone's out, the few people that are unfold their stylish umbrellas when it's time to step out from cover. The smart shops are empty, in the doorway of a chemists a pharmacist is smoking a cigarette.

The leaning tower of Pisa is beautiful beneath storm clouds, with just a few onlookers under umbrellas it looks proud and resilient. We walk around it, looking at it from different angles, from the south side the wet stone concourse reflects the tower and the cathedral like a mirror.

Restaurants in this part of town are quiet tonight, waiters hang around doorways, poised with menus like fishing bait, ready to reel passing customers in. There aren't any. At one of them a group of waiting staff have given up, sat with their elbows on a table by the window while the rain falls outside. We're hungry but there's no way we're going into one of these places, we need something local, the centre of Pisa is not where we'll find it.

Body heat is making our clothes damp beneath our waterproofs. There's nowhere obvious to eat on this side of the bridge so we make our way back to the van. Just a stone's throw from where we've played is a pizzeria we've never noticed before. The front door's all steamed up but we can see enough to know it's full of locals. Counter service, you just grab a free table, there's one left by the entrance. We hang our waterproofs on the back of our chairs, the steam rising off them adding to the moisture already accumulated on the front windows and doors.

Three guys in white aprons are busy behind the counter, two of them stretching out pizzas, feeding them into a massive wood fired oven while the other takes the orders. I'm not even sure if he's heard what I've said, he seemed to start serving the next customer before I'd even finished ordering. Two minutes later and I'm handed two hot plates and two drinks.

We go to Livorno one last time, it's Monday, washing day across the city. Apartment blocks with clothes lines strung from balconies and windows, a rainbow of linen and laundry like bunting. We'll soon be able to have clean clothes ourselves too, any day of the week. It's so much colder now, even when the sun is shining, the true late November weather is starting to show itself. It's time to leave, we can feel it and we resolve to go tomorrow, after the rush hour traffic has calmed down.

We head up the coastal highway, back the way we came when we drove down to Lucca a few weeks ago, seems like months ago now, back past

La Spezia and the Cinque Terre. By noon we're ready for a break and come off the motorway at Chiavari. Parking up on the beach front, taking the short walk into town. It's nearly one o'clock, everything's closing for lunch. A bakery is busy with the last rush of customers, that's a good sign. Inside behind the serving counters are rows of baskets filled with focaccia. They look good and by the queue at the counter the Italians think so too. We take a number and when it's called out make some hasty choices, one with onions, a plain one, another with sun dried tomatoes. They weigh the slices and pack them neatly in little grease proof bags.

Lots of empty benches along the promenade between olive and palm trees, plenty of places to sit, rip open our oily paper bags and divide up the bread. The restaurants on the waterfront are all closed, this is a town in winter repose. On the beach there's a large collection of rowing boats in blue and white striped covers, sleeping their way through the slow and quiet months in their winter pyjamas.

We drive back past Genoa, the last big metropolis on the coast this side of the French border. Still a hundred miles of Italian motorway to go, cutting along and through steep hills and rocks, endless tunnels. Past terraces built into vertical hillsides, houses perched on the sides of mountains that look impossible to access. Far below us the coastal towns and villages, the Ligurian Sea, the sun always seems to be shining when we drive along here.

We're not ready to leave Italy yet. A couple of miles before the border we come off the motorway at Ventimiglia, the last Italian town before you cross into France. The road bends back on itself, loops round off the motorway and sends us down to the centre of town and the sea. There's a long straight beach front running parallel to the town, tall palm trees at intervals along a pink pavement, grey and white pebbles on the beach. Cars parked all along the road, no spaces, but further out there's a few and we tuck in between a couple of cars, it feels fine to stay overnight.

Once the sun has come up the next morning, after it's warmed the van, taken off the night chill and lifted the condensation, we sit sideways on the bed with our coffee looking out over the water. Only the occasional runner or dog walker comes by, no one notices we're sat in the back. As a last farewell to Italy we load up our busking trolley and take it into town to see if there's anywhere we can play.

Ventimiglia's locals are out shopping in good numbers but there's no pedestrian areas that we can find. A few spots in front of some shops but they're all on pavements by roads where we'd be up against the sound of traffic. As we're circling round the middle of town we come to a large open entrance to a building, a doorway big enough to drive a truck through, people coming in and out. My eyes take a second to adjust to the change of light as we walk through, a market place, fruit and vegetable stalls in rows to our left, permanent shops around the edge. Sunlight is shining through the opposite door straight ahead, the exit to the neighbouring street. To our right is an open space in front of a shop, a fishmongers, raised up a few feet, white aprons moving around inside, weighing and bagging up fish for a constant flow of customers going up and down it's steps.

"What do you think?"

I'm asking but we both know it's either here or nowhere. Jayne thinks we should just get on with it, she's braver than me, I want to ask for permission. I go inside, there's a column in the centre of the shop, covered in a ceramic seascape, green fish swim on waves scratched in lines on the surface. The walls are tiled blue, white and grey, long steel counters full of ice, packed with every type of creature from the sea. Fishes eyes, staring out, staring up at the waving, gesturing and pointing going on above them.

I go up to the oldest guy behind the counter, he isn't serving, just telling others what to do. He's got the look of authority, the wear and tear in his face of a lifetime in the business. I ask him if it's okay to play some music outside the shop, he shrugs in the affirmative, he's got better things to do.

We set up and play. People shopping for fruit and vegetables have their purses out, spare change in their hands. They're already halfway there if they like what we do and it's easy for them to let a coin or two slip out of their palm and into the guitar case. Over to our left by the side of the big entrance are some guys drinking coffee at some tables and chairs. They're sat looking at us, stony faced, surly, drinking from tiny little coffee cups, their deadpan expressions never change. One of them is dressed very fine, even for an Italian at a grocery market, a white silk scarf and trilby hat, an expensive overcoat, occasionally a guy leans over and says something into his ear as they continue to look at us.

After half an hour the smart guy gets up and goes back outside to the cafe where the coffee cups come from. A minute later he's here again, walking towards us, purposeful, then dipping his head slightly, a brief gesture as he puts a five euro note in our case. Gradually the other guys follow, dropping coins in on their way past, making the same gesture as they leave.

Next morning the temperature drops, ice on the windows when we wake up, it's freezing, we have to run the engine, get the heater to clear the windscreen before we can set off into France. Jayne's behind the wheel ready to drive as soon as there's visibility through the window. While the engine slowly shares it's heat with us, I look at the options of somewhere to stay, cold fingers tapping on the cold screen of a phone, trying to find somewhere cheap, somewhere not far from our destination. Three nights to go until the house sit starts, we need a warm place and a hot bath, probably several. The best deal I can find is a hotel outside the centre of Narbonne, it's going to take the best part of five hours to get there.

The roads are fast and clear, we've a one track mind, a sole purpose as Jayne motors us towards our goal, to get clean and be warm.

We make good time, by about three in the afternoon we're pulling off the motorway, a couple of turns and we're in an industrial area on the edge of town, driving into the hotel's car park, there are no other cars in it.

Through the front doors there's a big reception area. Mostly empty except for a round glass topped table surrounded by wicker chairs with solid square cushions in them, it looks like garden furniture, weather proof. Plastic plants in pots in the corners. I ring the bell at the desk and an older guy in a cardigan with heavy rimmed spectacles comes out of an office at the back. He checks us in and we follow the stairs up to the next floor, make our way along two lengthy corridors past more plastic plants. No sign of any other guests.

The room is functional. It'll be okay once we get clean then get some food inside us, our little home for three nights. I run the bath, holding my hand under the stream of water from the tap, waiting for it to get hot. Waiting some more. I try moving my hand closer to the spout, then further away, then close again. Check that it's definitely the hot tap I'm running. Yes, the other one's absolutely freezing. I wait longer, pushing my fingers inside, can I feel some warmth coming through? Sometimes I think so but no. Jayne puts her head round the bathroom door,

"How is it?"

It's bad news, no matter how long I run the tap the water's lukewarm. We become agitated, pacing around our unpacked bags on the floor, the room closes in on us and feels darker.

I go down to reception, the man comes out from the back office again and up to the desk, I tell him the problem. He takes his spectacles off, a single motion that slides them off his face and places them upside down on the counter. My French teacher used to do exactly the same thing, this guy also follows the gesture up by massaging the bridge of his nose. He then explains they don't run the boiler too high this time of year because there's only a few guests. Putting his glasses back on, he comes out and walks over to a nearby door. He disappears inside for a second, I can't see where, then he's back in the doorway, says he's turned it up a bit and for us to wait half an hour and try again.

We wait forty five minutes. I run the tap again, holding my fingers next to the spout, then further away, then close again, waiting. No change, just a steady stream of lukewarm water. With the plug in, the bath starts to fill but the water that accumulates is cold.

Three nights we've got booked here, we take our unpacked bags down to reception, tell him we want to cancel the reservation and leave. The guy gives us a shrug, a downturned mouth, taking his spectacles off and laying them on the counter again. He only works here, the owners won't be happy, they might refund the next two nights but not tonight. We explain we're not happy either, the only thing we've done in the room is put cold water in the bath, it's probably cleaner than when we arrived! We'd like a full refund, the reservation is through a hotel booking website so we'll cancel it ourselves online and write to tell them the reason, explain how unhappy we are. He shrugs again as we walk out, says we can try.

In the front seat of the van we start searching for accommodation all over again. A little after five o'clock now, the sun setting, cold and dark outside and a mood to match inside. We're looking for guarantees. For an extra twenty euros a night there's a hotel chain half a kilometre away, twenty more euros has got to buy warmer water and a nicer room, we book it and drive round. There's other cars in the car park, automatic doors at the entrance effortlessly glide open, warm ceiling lamps glowing like pumpkins light up the reception desk.

One hour later and we're wrapped in big white towels lying on the bed, our skin red from soaking in boiling hot water, body and limbs heavy from the heat, euphoric and exhausted.

Three nights in one place, not moving or driving, not finding somewhere to sleep or busking. We buy cold drinks to put in the mini bar, baguettes and croissants from the nearby bakery, shake the crumbs off the duvet from eating picnics on the bed. Twenty four hour hot water means we can take a shower, then run the bath and luxuriate in the pure water straight after. Someone told me it's what the Japanese do, shower first then lie in crystal clear hot water, that way you avoid immersing yourself in the dirt you've just washed off. It feels very zen. The bath doubles as a washing machine, Jayne cleans us a set of clothes to wear for when we turn up at the house sit, the room temperature's high enough to dry them overnight.

The centre of Narbonne sits on two sides of a canal with wide footpaths and there's a huge Gothic cathedral. The stone buildings and piazzas in town have a white hue about them and the wind whips through the open spaces, it feels cold enough to snow at the moment. We walk through a small park that's been yarn bombed, the trees completely wrapped from top to bottom in knitting, trunks and branches all in their own crocheted, multicoloured sleeves. Bright balls of woolly knitted pom-poms hang from them like winter fruits, the park is called the Garden of the Martyrs of the Resistance.

The hotel booking website gets back to us, says the other hotel will refund us the whole three nights. When it's time to leave we drive past it on our way out, there are still no cars in the car park.

Our house-sit is in a small town only twenty miles away, a short easy drive along straight roads, past acres of vineyards and flat fields, wind turbines in the distance. The road climbs as we get closer to the village and the plains fall away.

A wide avenue runs through the centre of Azille, big enough for a tree-lined walkway in the middle and the road to pass on either of it's sides. Grey and sandy coloured houses line the street, some shutters are brown, some are blue, they're all closed. There's a bar, a couple of people sat inside, also a boulangerie and a little local shop. A population of about a thousand when we looked it up, there's a post office and a winery, we might have everything we need right here.

The house we're going to is off the main avenue down a street where front doors open straight onto the road. Three storey sandy coloured houses, more closed shutters apart from our one, bustling activity going on inside when we arrive. A young family getting ready to go back to England, an early Christmas trip to see relatives and friends, bags of presents in the hallway, lots of luggage. They make us very welcome and are glad to see us, glad we've got here, that we've come to look after their little dog Ralph. Also their cat, hamster and goldfish.

They show us to our room on the top floor, a cosy little attic bedroom with a sloping roof, we leave our bags there and go back downstairs. There's an adjoining lounge and kitchen area with a log burner. Ralph jumps on our laps as we're sat on the sofa while the family carry on packing, making last minute phone calls, crossing off things on the to do list. Ralph's a little black shaggy haired poodle, a small dog with nervous energy, happy to get attention from anyone available, he knows there's something going on. He jumps off the sofa briefly in the final flurry of activity when they leave but then he's straight back up on our laps.

Quiet descends on the house, Ralph's small warm body is trembling between us. With one hand each on him, we sit in silence on the sofa, only the sound of a clock ticking somewhere in the room. Ralph lies down, licks Jayne's hand. I can see the kitchen from where I'm sat, the oven, the kettle, the pots and pans, the dishwasher. Homely features, all mod cons and facilities available to us whenever we want them. Eighteen whole days.

Azille sits on the top of a hill surrounded by vineyards, perfect for dog walks. We can pretty much set off in any direction and the town soon gives way to open fields and countryside. Ralph can be let off the lead once we're out of the centre of town and in the open, he loves running in rings around us. His curly black hair bobs up and down in rhythm with his little legs. He gets excited when he's charging around but his smart poodle brain will always kick in and he'll come to a sudden stop, look around to check where we are, then bound off again.

Most mornings there's a frost on the ground and more often than not a clear blue sky overhead. There are walnut and almond trees on the edges of the vineyards, small farm houses with stacks of chopped wood by the front door and a steady stream of smoke coming from their chimneys. Any number of paths take us around the village and we can make our way back in from wherever we end up, back past the closed shutters, the town hushed and still. Hardly anyone around, only an occasional *bonjour* with a passer by breaks the silence.

The boulangerie is open every morning, we always let the paths lead us to it on the way back. Most days there are a few croissants left and we get two to have with our coffee, we always buy a baguette. Some of the locals come out of the shop with large clusters of them, big bags with them all sticking out like an archer's quiver full of bread arrows. Are there meals that need that many baguettes? Maybe there are large extended families living behind all those closed shutters.

A routine of sorts develops, walking the dog, having breakfast, working on songs, rehearsing. After lunch we try to get more bookings for next year, send emails, apply to festivals, try to get more gigs for New Zealand in the new year. So many gaps in the diary after that, no matter what bookings come in, it's the gaps we keep looking at. Then we take Ralph out again, a final walk before dark and it's time to light the log burner.

I've always been a good sleeper, I can go to bed anytime and get my head down for eight hours. Jayne's body clock is more irregular, she goes through phases where she can't sleep, sitting up in bed working in the middle of the night. I'll roll over and see her face illuminated by the screen of her iPad, intent, focussed, tapping out emails. Next morning she'll be dead to the world and only strong coffee and Ralph's energetic anticipation of going for a walk will wake her.

There must be other people up at that time of night though, judging by some of the responses she gets back. A lot of good things can happen in the small hours, most of our gigs for example. As she's sipping her first coffee I know there's some good news when she says,

"Guess what?"

Then she'll tell me of a late night exchange, a back and forth of emails resulting in a booking.

We're thinking about where we'll go next, for Christmas, New Year and most of January. When we're out walking around the vineyards, Jayne says,

"If you could chose anywhere to house-sit, where would it be?"

That's a good question. Further south might be good, it might be warmer, perhaps a couple of cats for a change. I make sure Ralph is out of earshot, he's busy working his way along a row of vines, weaving in and out. We talk about ideal scenarios, penthouse suites, beach front properties, swimming pools.

A few days later and Jayne has another middle of the night session. When I bring coffee in the morning she opens her eyes, sits up slowly,

"You never guess what?"

Ralph and I wait on the bed expectantly.

"A German couple in Spain want us to look after their cats over Christmas and New Year."

It's in Andalusia, about 30 miles north of Malaga. They need us to get there the day after we finish here, around seven hundred and fifty miles south.

The day before the homeowners come back we clean the house and pack our bags. Once we start, Jayne wants to leave, she's itching to go. Stems from her childhood, her father was in the RAF, they moved around, different places, new barracks, new houses, new schools, new towns. Once the winds of change start blowing she wants out, she just wants to go, get on with it, leave where we are behind. But we have to wait, poised and ready.

Our family arrive back in the morning, filling the hallway with suitcases, bags of Christmas presents they've received, the same amount as they took with them to give. Ralph sniffs around, putting his nose in the open bags in between getting fussed over. We say goodbye, but not to Ralph, we don't want to excite him further or get too sad ourselves. Then we side step our way around the luggage and out of the front door.

There's a couple of routes we can take and we opt to go down the coast to Valencia before the road turns inland. Driving and driving all day, by the early evening we've arrived at Valencia. We need a break to stretch our legs, the city is alive with throngs of people out shopping, busy streets lined with the twinkling frosty white lights of Christmas. The open doors of the bigger shops blast you with warm air and seasonal music, if it isn't music it's the sound of sleigh bells.

We drive just a little further in the evening

and stop overnight at what looks to be a highway service area. There's a couple of fuel pumps and a cafeteria, the lights are all off and it's closed. All is quiet when we lay down in the back and go to sleep.

When I wake up there are sounds outside, Spanish voices, a car door slams. Peeking through the curtains, bright sunlight, the forecourt full of cars, the cafe is busy, it's front door permanently open. We get dressed and quietly open the side door of the van, the ground is dusty.

Inside the cafe the walls are pink, the floor a soft yellow, the tables and chairs silver and chrome. Light bounces around the room blending the colours into one, like a candyfloss dream. We order coffee, a euro each, served with the biggest bulging sachet of sugar I've ever seen. The coffee's strong, there's only just enough room in the cup to get the sugar in, I can feel the spoon dredging through the sludge of granules in the bottom. Then the final dregs of undissolved sugar with the last sip, sweetness and bitterness competing for who will be remembered last.

Our destination is Antequera, we've got instructions on the best place to park when we get there. The couple live in an apartment in the centre of town, on the first floor above some shops on a pedestrian street. They say to leave the van a mile away by a small park behind the bullring. There are other cars parked up but it's easy enough to find a space. We grab an overnight bag and our instruments and cut down through the paths that criss-cross the gardens at the back of the bullring, the Plaza de Toros. It's a huge white and brown bricked amphitheatre that dominates the small roundabout at the edge of town.

Up the main street and the town comes to life with shops, bars and restaurants. It's the end of the afternoon but the sun is out in a blanket of blue sky and there are customers in winter clothes sat outside with drinks and tapas. Antequera feels Spanish and local, we might be only thirty miles from Malaga but there's no sign of a happy hour or egg and chips anywhere. A smaller street leads at an angle off the main road, a one way thoroughfare, small local clothing and fashion shops, a green grocer, children's shoes, a toy store. Then past a restored art deco cinema painted bright blue, white and red before we turn into our home street. A marble floored alley, a higher end parade of boutiques, a perfumery, pharmacist, an opticians, some expensive clothes outlets. Halfway up and we're there, pressing the bell and being buzzed through the iron door, then up the open staircase to the first floor, this is us.

Walter and Susanne are German but speak perfect English, they've retired here and say it's cheap to live in this part of Spain. They let us settle in then take us to a local bar where they know the owner well, it sounds like their Spanish is excellent too. We have a few drinks and try some tapas, Susanne says no matter what they eat or drink it never comes to more than twenty euros.

Later we go back to the apartment, I drink tea while the others have a nightcap. Walter used to own a boat back in Germany, a tall ship, a historical artefact. They ran adventure holidays, educational excursions where they taught young people to sail. Both of them talk fondly about it and show us photographs, Walter and Susanne sat around a galley table surrounded by red faced smiling young adults. They miss it, it was a wrench to sell it but the passage of time was catching up with them. Walter is a little older than Susanne and they've come to Spain for warmer weather and a new life on land.

Susanne recycles umbrellas, broken ones she finds around town. She brings them back to life, 'dead umbrellas' she calls them when they're lying in the street. With the material she makes little handmade bags, all shapes and sizes, a variety of patterns and colours, neatly sewn together and waterproof. Some she keeps, others she sells or gives as gifts to friends. I can't think if I've seen many discarded umbrellas,

"Are there a lot of them lying around?"

"They're everywhere."

The apartment is long and runs lengthways away from the street. A sitting room at the front, lined with shelves, large books in German and English, atlases, encyclopedias, volumes on art, history and travel. There's a dining table, a small sofa at one end and French doors that open onto a tiny balcony overlooking the shops. They have a gas fire in the front room for this time of year, one of those free standing ones you have to hold the button down for ages until the pilot light ignites the grill panels.

Behind the front room is a small kitchen then a long corridor lined with more book shelves that takes you to the back of the apartment, our bedroom and two bathrooms. One for us and one for the two cats, Moritz and Sophia and their litter trays.

In the morning before Walter and Susanne leave we all sit together around the dining table for breakfast. Bread and jam, fruit and yoghurt. After Walter has finished his yoghurt he breaks into a smile, then begins to call out,

"Moritz."

Then louder,

"Moritz!"

His voice is persistent, then louder still,

"Mooooooritz!"

The black and white cat eventually appears from the hallway, rubbing the side of his back on the door frame before hurrying over. Walter lowers the yogurt pot to ground level for Moritz to lick around the insides, rotating it slowly until it's all clean,

"Any particular flavour?" I ask,

"He likes them all."

Then they need to make a move, a long journey, a bus to catch and a train to Portugal. They're house sitting for friends with a whole bunch of animals, somewhere very rural. They've been before and wanted to help their friends out and have a change of scene this winter. They put their rucksacks on as we all say our goodbyes, the farewells tagged onto Christmas and New Year's good wishes. Then they're gone, closing the front door of the apartment behind them. Quiet. Once again the silence of someone else's home descends around us.

Antequera is a great town for walking, all sorts of ways to lose ourselves in discovery, we can let it unfold more every time we go out. Up on the hill is an eleventh century fortress built by the Moors, the steps up there take us to panoramic views, the sun scorched hills and rocky outcrops in the distance. Views over the whole city too, chapels and churches everywhere. We never need to walk the same way twice and often find places we don't recognise before turning a corner back into somewhere familiar.

Broken umbrellas appear on the streets, most days we see at least one, they're on our radar now and we're tuned in to find them. In gutters, lying on pavements or sticking out of dustbins like wonky aerials. Others are splattered and splayed out on the road, like they've been thrown to the ground in disgust at having failed their owner.

Maybe it's because they're unnecessary, it never seems to rain much while we're here. Like Susanne said, it's cheap to live too. There's a green grocer around the corner, always busy with people, counters piled high with huge oranges and lemons, local produce, everything's from Spain. We come out with a big shopping bag full of fruit and vegetables, it never costs more than five euros.

One day before Christmas a small group gathers to sing songs in the street below. The happy music draws us down from the apartment, there's some conga drums and two guitar players, the singers are all smiling and clapping along. Friends appear, mingling with the audience, those in the group that know them step out when they arrive and give them big *"ola"* and a hug before rejoining the singing.

On Boxing Day we lose one of the cats. They've been raised as indoor cats and always stay in the apartment. Moritz is easy to find, we saw him at breakfast this morning for his yoghurt, he's usually not too far away. Sophia on the other hand keeps herself to herself and is nowhere to be seen. Could she have got on the balcony and jumped down to the street? The French door's only open occasionally and we keep a close eye on it. We go through every room, she's nowhere. Then we go through again, banging a saucepan with a wooden spoon in the hope of flushing her out. Nothing. We look over the balcony, then go down to the street. Nothing. What can we do? Where is she? Once more with a fine tooth comb through every inch of every room. Approaching despair, and at the end of trying every conceivable place, when there, on a high shelf of an out of the way cupboard tucked behind a pile of towels we see her little ears. She raises her head, looks at us, our wide eyed relieved faces peering in at her, then lowers her head and goes back to sleep.

There's an evening concert in a local church, Bach's Christmas Oratorio. The chapel is full, woolly winter overcoats filling every seat, we just squeeze onto the end of a pew. The roof is so high that the building is more tall than it is long, like it's built on it's end. My eyes are drawn upwards, it's like vertigo in reverse, continually pulling my attention up to the far away rafters. When the choir starts singing the serenity of the voices and harmonies gives even more of an uplift, raising me up to the heavenly vaults. Maybe that's why they built it so high, so that when a choir sings you've got somewhere to go.

The biggest event of them all is the Epiphany, the Three Kings Day, *El Día de los Reyes Magos*, the sixth of January. A celebration of the arrival of the three wise men in Bethlehem. It's crazy on the streets, there's thousands out lining the roads for a huge parade. We're on the main street, amongst a population in a joyous and festive mood, decorated floats coming by, people in gloriously colourful costumes. Anything goes, characters from Disney, glittering suits and sequins, biblical scenes, a pageant for the world.

I feel something hit my head, a small hard object, then again, what the hell is it? Everyone around me is clambering around. Sweets! Showers of them thrown from the trucks, raining down like missiles on the excited crowd. A hail storm of candy, huge cheers go up every time and we fill our pockets until they're bulging.

A short drive out of town is El Torcal de

Antequera. Walter and Susanne have said we have to go and visit. It's a nature reserve in the mountains, there's a visitor's centre, a car park and easy hiking trails. Driving in and parking up is like entering an alien landscape. Huge towers of pancake rocks, impossibly balanced on top of each other, layers of eroded stacks of limestone in a dessert. We walk around it all afternoon, clambering around these strange and beautiful formations resolving to come back the next day and make a video. A video for one of our songs, 'Take It With You When You Go'. A song about what things it might be important to keep as we transferred our life from a one bedroom flat to living on the road. It starts like this:

You know I collected some sunshine
Found a way to catch rain
Put it all in a Chinese jar
Will you take it with you when you go

Been listening to the sound of the rushes
Making friends with the breeze
Throwing them all in a suitcase
Will you take them with you when you go

Don't think I could've forgotten
I think you've got it all
But if there's ever something you need
You know who to call

Stumbled over a mountain

Skimmed it over the sea
Stuffed it all in a paper cup
Will you take it with you when you go

Been busy capturing footprints
Saving all of my dreams
Cutting them all into pieces
Will you take them with you when you go

Then Susanne calls with some bad news. Walter has fallen down the stairs in the house they're looking after and has been taken to a nearby hospital. She's tearful and hopes he won't be in too long, she's been with him all day but has had to go back overnight to take care of the animals.

The next day she calls again. Unbelievably sad news, shocking. Walter has passed away in hospital. She wasn't there at the time and the doctors and nurses did everything they could but couldn't save him, she's distraught and doesn't know what she's going to do.

Time slows, the apartment feels darker, quieter, so different. Walter is here, everywhere around us, in his books, pictures and memorabilia, it doesn't seem real that he won't be coming back. Susanne calls again the next day. She's unable to hold back the tears, asking if we can stay a bit longer. Walter is going to be cremated and she and his son will make a pilgrimage to Germany to scatter his ashes. Can we wait another week? We tell her it's no problem, we can stay longer.

When she arrives home she looks tired, older, her life changed so completely since we last saw her. We sit and talk about Walter, their life on sea together and the life they'd started to build here. She knows she has a new life to build now, not the one she'd originally thought. As we get ready to leave she says,

"Where are you going now?

"Cadiz."

There's a few days before we make our way back to England. We've always thought of Cadiz as a place we might go this winter, somewhere if all else fails, a safety net. Ever since someone said it would be warm enough to camp we've had it in mind. We just want to see it now, might as well, it's only a couple of hours away. Susanne says if we're going to go there then we must go to Ronda on the way. After sad goodbyes we walk one last time through the streets of Antequera, out of the centre to the edge of town, round the other side of the bullring to our van parked up beneath the trees and then we're back on the road again.

Ronda is spectacular, built in the mountains on top of near vertical rocks. The town is split in half by a steep gorge and a river, the two sides connected by three bridges. The biggest one is one hundred and twenty metres above the canyon floor. It looks like it's carved out of the very rock and stone that it's built on, or that the mountains have eroded away to reveal a beautiful arched bridge. We line up with Japanese tourists at the sightseeing spots and take photos.

By the early evening we've made it to Cadiz, a long headland sticking out of the coast seventy miles west of the southern tip of Spain. A sea port, heavily built up, turns out it's one of the oldest cities in Western Europe, people have been living here for more than three thousand years. The eastern side is the industrial shipping port and ferry terminal but the western strip has a beach and we squeeze into a space where there's roadside parking and walk into the old town. It's protected by imposing city walls, a wide fortified entrance big enough to allow multiple lanes of traffic in and out. Once you're through though it's easy to disappear into endless winding alleyways, a rabbit warren of small side streets that connect the city's plazas and piazzas. The wrong time of year to look for somewhere to eat, lots of empty tourist restaurants. I can see too much tablecloth, too many waiters looking at their watches.

We sleep the night on the beach front but one night is enough and it's time to move out of the city. Round the headland on the other side of the bay is El Puerto de Santa Maria, there's a campsite near the sea. It has a kind of holiday park entrance, little red flags on top of white wooden buildings, a barrier at the gate as we drive through. This time of year though this is no holiday park. The residents of the site are exactly that, residents, they're not holiday makers, this is January, these are people here for the winter.

If feels like it too, like everyone's doing their time, waiting. In the late morning of the second day it's warm enough to sit outside the van and play our instruments. A guy comes over, I'm thinking maybe he plays guitar or likes music and is coming to say hi, but no, he says,

"You might like listening to what you're playing but I don't."

So although we've checked in for a few nights we spend most of it walking along the coastline. Whenever we feel like playing music, we go to the beach, sit on the steps and serenade the palm trees that are growing on the wide expanse of beautiful and empty sand dunes. A wind swept barren landscape, a contrast to the busy port of Cadiz we can see in the distance a mile across the sea.

We did end up coming south for the winter. It's a unique feeling, travelling for the purpose of staying warm. Always on our minds, migration, flight and freedom, birds. We write a song on the steps of the beach, 'Turnstone', after the coastal, migratory birds that feed and scavenge on beaches and fly south for the winter.

> *Turnstone, fly me home*
> *Take me on your wing*
> *I know we'll shake it out*
> *Whatever winter brings*
>
> *Clearwings are flying*
> *They're following the streams*

They know that nights are cold
And gathering

Swallow I know you know
How to find your way
I'll see you in the south
On that sunny day

Blackbird, I have heard
A song sets you free
Maybe fly a little slow
And wait for me

Old crows and shadows
Know that time
Is just a flyway
To leave it all behind

Silver shells and feathers
Jewels in the sand
Smoke on the mountain
Across the land

Then, like every migrating bird, we turn around and head back home again.

8. THE LAND OF THE LONG WHITE CLOUD

At Auckland airport our tired eyes are blinking in their first proper exposure to daylight for two days. New Zealand summertime, we've lost a night's sleep on the long flight from a London winter. A six hour stop over in Dubai in the middle of the night, already tired by the time we got there, doubly so knowing we had another eleven hour flight still to go. Sleep wasn't for the want of trying. There were yellow sloping recliners on one of the concourses at Dubai airport, all taken, we kept walking past until two became free. Then we lay back ready to rest but the seats were made of slippery plastic and I kept sliding down, Jayne too. Other people didn't have this problem, their eyes were closed, faces peaceful, hands resting gently together on their laps. Our hands couldn't rest on our laps, we had to use them to prop ourselves up, arms held rigid to keep us in place, legs pushing out like an exercise machine. Maybe it took practice, we gave up and went to lie on the floor of a large canteen behind a sign saying it was closed for the night.

A minibus picks us up at the airport to go and collect our rental car, the cheapest one we can get, no insurance. The young smart guy that serves us is breezy and upbeat, he takes us around the outside of our vehicle with a clipboard noting the scratches, bumps and marks that are already on it, cheerfully writing them down like they're optional extras.

"Dent in the centre of the rear number plate."

"Scratch along the drivers door below the handle."

I sign the sheet and agree to the descriptions of damaged bodywork next to a diagram of the car covered in x's that show where they are. Fingers crossed there aren't any more by the time we bring it back, he takes the clipboard, hands us the keys and gives us our first, 'Awesome'.

We drive into the suburbs of Auckland, we have hosts for our first night, a welcoming home to head to. Gillian and Arthur, long time friends of my dad and stepmum, they moved here from the UK decades ago. When they heard we were coming they were quick to invite us to stay.

Arthur is a tall bear of a guy with a sailor's beard like Captain Haddock, happy to turn any conversation into banter. Gillian is kind and motherly but with a maths professor's brain ticking away behind large round glasses, she teaches at the university. They have a dog called Bob.

There's a pot of coffee waiting in the kitchen, afterwards to keep from falling asleep, we take

Bob for a walk with Gillian. They live on a quiet street in a leafy suburb, a block away from a hill, an ancestral mountain. Auckland is mostly a flat landscape, dotted here and there with old volcanoes, hills that suddenly rise up out of the land. Bob leads us to the top, we're lagging behind his wagging tail as the path gets steeper at the summit. We can see the suburbs below, a dense patchwork of wooden houses and green trees, miles and miles of it. In the distance is Mount Eden, another old volcano and Auckland's biggest. Beyond that the city itself and it's most famous landmark, the Sky Tower, high above everything else on the horizon.

"I hope the television didn't keep you awake last night?"

Our first morning and Arthur's pouring us fresh coffee from a percolator that seems to be on most of the time. Always gently gurgling and hissing away, the centre piece of their kitchen, radiating a warm fragrance.

"Not a chance."

We stayed up as long as we could, saw the British segment that comes at the end of the television news then crashed out. Our bed is the other side of double doors that open into the lounge but we didn't hear a thing and must have been asleep for twelve hours.

Arthur says to help ourselves to breakfast,

toast, whatever we want and proudly shows us his jar of Marmite,

"Marmageddon is over."

It was unavailable for over a year, there were production problems after the Christchurch earthquake, it's back on the shelves now.

"So, when's your first gig?"

The caffeine's starting to circulate in my bloodstream,

"Tomorrow night!"

Maybe another cup to get the day started, overpower the fuzziness, get our heads around going to play a gig.

We get our instruments out, check them over from the long haul flight. For safety they travel with the strings slack and unwound. As I wind the tension back in I feel like one of the strings myself, coffee and the thought of a concert tomorrow night bringing me back into tune.

Our first gig's in a western suburb of Auckland only twenty minutes out of the city. Titirangi, we're told the locals here are known as "Westies", an artistic community, a more bohemian lifestyle. We're the guests at a folk club that meet at the village hall right on the waterfront of Paturoa Bay. Driving down to the beach we pass a wooden sign advertising yoga, another for pottery classes, houses tucked away in a thick forest, joined to the road by quirky driveways, all shapes and sizes. Auckland is a relaxed city but the pace of life feels even slower here.

At the bottom the road opens out into a perfect little horseshoe bay, there's a small empty car park, manicured grass and a children's play area. We get out and walk onto the beach, standing by the shoreline a woman is holding a multicoloured umbrella looking out at the bay as a kayak rows past. The setting is beautiful, I move up closer and take a photograph. Seconds later she turns around, smiles at us both and walks away.

The Beach Hall is set back a little from the waterfront where the treeline begins, well maintained and painted a dark blue grey. Inside it has pristine wooden floors, a proper stage at one end. Early evening and people start arriving on foot and in cars, the room fills with an eager crowd, some with instrument cases. They play songs in the first half and then we play after the interval. At the end we get introduced to Bevis who'll put us up for the night.

I think I'm meeting my first true 'Westy'. Bevis is laid back, shoulder length red hair, a beard, wearing an open neck shirt, shorts and sandals. He lives a stone's throw from the club and we walk back together in the dark, a few friends come along and we sit up until the early hours drinking, swapping songs and jamming. Bevis says our life reminds him of a song he's written and he plays it for us. 'Dancing with the Road', a jaunty folk song with a catchy chorus, his rolling fingerpicking carrying it along on the guitar. Journeys and a longing to travel, the words are full of a yearning to get out on the road.

Breakfast the next morning and Bevis makes us avocado and tomatoes on toast drizzled with extra virgin olive oil. I don't know if this is a "Westy" thing but it tastes good, the avocado spreads like a thick butter over the toast, salt and pepper pull the juice out of the fresh ripe tomatoes and the oil mixes it all together.

Then we're drinking more coffee and have the guitars out again. Bevis starts playing an Irish tune, round and round it goes, the energy and infectiousness building. It worms it's way into our ears and we make him teach it to us. 'Morrison's Jig', our first ever Irish tune and we've come to New Zealand to learn it! We go over and over it, there are two parts, both played twice every time, a linking motif that brings you back to the beginning and you're off again. Bevis stays patient until we have it and are joining in, a little slower at first, we keep going, none of us can stop.

Midday and we need to leave, my ears ringing with 'Morrison's Jig' on repeat. We thank Bevis for his hospitality, education in sophisticated breakfasts and the Irish music lesson and head off, dancing with the road.

A gig in the afternoon at a funky bar on a crossroads in the Ponsonby area of Auckland. Run by Matthew, young, charming, wearing a t-shirt underneath an unbuttoned short sleeve shirt. He's dressed casually but there's no mistaking the business mind whirring away inside. The Golden Dawn opened as a pop up bar a year ago and has kept going, getting a reputation as a place to come for the vibe and the music. The weathers good, we play on the terrace, the chilled out Sunday Auckland crowd happy to drink their way through the afternoon.

A man comes over to say hi in the break. Rick, sunglasses and neatly trimmed white goatee beard, white shoulder length hair coming out of a straw hat. Young at heart. He's very complementary, an instant friend and he says to let him know when we're playing again and he'll come and see us. Rick plays guitar too, writes his own songs. His daughter's in the music business, she goes by the name of Aldous Harding. Afterwards we look her up, she's young, beautiful and different, very cool and set to get very big.

Our next gig is north in the The Bay of Islands but not for a couple of days, we've got the time to go further up, do a road trip to the most northerly point, to Cape Reinga and Spirits Bay, around two hundred and fifty miles away. Highway 1 could take us all the way there, up the eastern side, but there's an option to take a detour along smaller roads on the west so we choose that. Through the Waipoua Forest, where the Tāne Mahuta is, a two thousand year old Kauri tree.

There's a lay-by nearby and a few cars parked up, just a short walk into the forest and there it is. Huge and magnificent, a giant towering above us, it's trunk alone is over fifteen metres all the way round. No photo can do it justice but everyone is trying to capture it on camera and I'm no different, standing on the boardwalk that's been built for viewing, neck strained upwards trying to get a photo. A photo of the 'Lord of the Forest'. It can't be done, you just get a photo of a tree.

So, like everyone does eventually, I stop trying and put the camera away. There are benches and we sit down, join others in quiet contemplation. The more I sit there, taking it in, the more this sacred space resonates, something you can feel, the presence, the beauty, the majesty.

That night we check into a backpackers lodge. It's cheap and the walls are thin. To avoid disturbing the neighbours we put socks underneath the strings on the guitar and ukulele and practice 'Morrison's Jig'. A muted clicking sound is all you can hear, like someone tapping away rhythmically on a computer keyboard. This much quieter version we rename 'Sock Morrisons'.

The next day we make it to the top of the Northland, to the tip of the Aupouri Peninsula, a sixty mile strip of land that sticks out between the Tasman Sea and the Pacific Ocean. There are no towns up here, the last one is seventy miles away, back before the peninsula even starts. Just one road to get you here, very few cars, no side roads or other destinations. We get stuck in a traffic jam for a short while with a herd of cows.

There's a wild campsite at Tapotupotu Bay right on the beach. Nearly two miles of track lead us down from the main road, the last few bends and I start to see the ocean and the sandy bay below.

A camping area, picnic tables and a few coloured tents pitched up for the night. It looks like heaven, a piece of paradise, we park up and chose a pitch with a great view out to sea. We've got a borrowed tent, a couple of sleeping bags, a stove and enough food, this place is so beautiful we think we'll stay for a couple of nights. The site's run on an honesty scheme, you put money into an envelope and post it in a wooden box. We drop the right amount of notes into the box for two nights.

A breeze picks up in the early evening as we're sat at the picnic table cooking and admiring the view. We put our jackets on and finish our meal, a little wind isn't going to deter us, it's part of the experience. Miles from civilization, miles from anywhere and it feels like it too. Zipped up in our waterproofs, the wind whistles past us, it's starting to churn up the sea, whipping up the sand. Out on the rocks there's a solitary tree growing, impossibly exposed to the elements, stubborn and resilient. Then the mosquitoes come and it's time to get in the tent and shut the front door.

In the middle of the night I wake up, Jayne's moving around,

"Where's the torch? Turn it on."

I switch it on, the beam lights up the shadows of hundreds of mosquitoes on the fabric of the tent. I'm thinking they're on the outside so I reach my hand out to flick them off the canvas but my fingers touch them, I can feel them. They're on the inside! They're everywhere!

Jayne is a hot blooded magnet for mosquitoes, they love her. If there's even one it'll bite her but here there' are hundreds and they're inside our tent. Now I've woken up I can feel the tightness of the skin on my face, pockets of heat and itchiness on my arms. We unzip the tent and hurry over to the car trailing our sleeping bags behind us and spend the rest of the night dozing on the front seats.

When dawn starts to break I can see Jayne's face covered in bites like she's got the measles, I try to reassure her,

"It doesn't look too bad."

It's time to move on, forget the second night. I wonder if I can prise our envelope with the money in it back out of the box? That's not going to look good, let it go. We've got to be in the Bay of Islands in a couple of days so we'll just head there, find somewhere to stay, a cheap backpackers, thin walls, sock Morrison's.

We drive south, three hours to Paihia, where our gig is. A pretty seaside town with a quaint harbour, a picture perfect tourist destination with souvenir shops, cafes and travel bureaus offering boat trips, cruises and tours. Everyone is out on the streets in sun hats and shades, shorts and sandals, carrying small knapsacks.

The gig is at a restaurant on the harbour, booked for late afternoon during happy hour. There's a corporate feel to the place, large and glass fronted, looking out over the water. Uniform chairs and tables on hard floors, lots of young waiting staff carrying trays of drinks and seafood platters, no sign of anyone in charge. We stop a waitress and tell her we're here to play music and are wondering where to set up,

"The dick."

It takes a second to register. We're playing outside, on the deck. More corporate furniture, outdoor heaters for the evening, a few couples and small groups sat at tables under large umbrellas. We set up to the side, people look over briefly, wondering what's about to happen, a guy lifts up his sunglasses squinting to see who we are more clearly. Then we play a set, little rounds of applause fade away quickly after each song, it feels like a soundtrack for table service. Music to watch waiters carry happy hour orders, trays of red and orange iced drinks with straws, bowls of fries and plates of fish go by. The kind of gig that half an hour after we've played it, as we're driving south to our next destination, I wonder if it even happened at all.

Gisborne is midway down the North Island on the east coast. As far as cities go, it's as east as you can get, the first place in the world to get the light of the sun rising on New Year's Day.

A gig at a winery. Another warm late summer day and we're playing outside again, this time on the grass. A beautiful chilled out afternoon, the breeze gently blowing through the vineyard, happy people eating and drinking wine, here to enjoy the music. The owner has done some good publicity, there's a picture of us in the local paper, the one of us holding the umbrella with the fairy lights all over it, the stars twinkling in the twilight. All the tables are booked. Jayne is happy too, it's a wine drinker's paradise, a promise of leaving with complementary bottles as a bonus for a full house.

In the break we get brought more drinks and a plate of food. There are small tables on the lawn facing us but over to the left there's also a long table under a marquee. A guy comes over from the group, soft spoken, a white flat top haircut, thick Buddy Holly glasses, introduces himself as Rowan,

"Would you like to come and join us for your break?"

We're welcomed into a large group of friends, smiling over glasses of wine and half finished plates of food. Smiling at us like we're part of the family, they genuinely want to know what we're up to,

"Where are you staying?"

We hadn't thought about it yet. Ian's asking, he's sat in the middle of the table with his wife Sheryl, they both have full heads of white hair. He's a teddy bear of a guy with a beard in an open necked summer shirt. Sheryl is petite, wearing green glasses and bright red lipstick, a wise owl look in her face.

"Come and stay at ours. We're going out tonight but you're welcome to make yourself at home. There's a hot tub."

Round the table we're all talking across each other, Jayne's in the chair beside me, talking to the lady next to her, animated. She's making the kind of cute noises that tell me she must be talking about dogs. Then she introduces me to Rowan's wife Lee, they have two Maltese terriers, they've invited us to their place tomorrow to meet them.

At the end of the gig, once we've packed up and collected our bottles of wine, we follow Sheryl and Ian in their car back to their house. As we go through the front door on their porch, there to the right, a cosy little room's made up, like they've been expecting us, fresh linen on a double bed.

Jayne's grandmother Elsie said the world was made of two types of people, either fluffy or tailored. Sheryl and Ian are fluffy, all soft edges and kindness,

"Help yourself to anything."

They're calling out through the open car window, waving as they head off for the evening. We're sat on the veranda, where we've been since we got here, just the two of us now. Actually three, they have a cat, Muffin, she's taken a liking to Jayne's lap. Her coat's a patchwork of white, black and grey, a brown stained face like she's dipped it in a milky teacup. Like us she doesn't want to be anywhere else either, curled up and happy, happy going nowhere.

We're still sat outside when they get back, late in the evening, picking up where we left off. Ian brings out some dessert wine, suggests Jayne tries it. If she likes it we can take a few bottles away with us, they have a surplus. They used to run a restaurant but now they're mostly retired, just a coffee truck as a sideline to take out at weekends. It's parked up in the backyard, they say they'll fire it up in the morning.

They do, and we're all back on the veranda, drinking good quality coffee in the shade of the warm New Zealand summer sun. Ian and Sheryl like to play music, they have lots of instruments around the house, mostly ukuleles that they play songs on together. Ian gets his ukulele and sings us the Tom Wait's song 'Chocolate Jesus'. The lyrics are tongue in cheek, about finding a chocolate Christ in a candy store, replacing the need to go to church or read the bible and pray. Ian relishes the message, sings the song with a straight face. Hot tubs, verandas, cats on laps, ukuleles and coffee, we've found our congregation. Not an easy place to leave either, we say a sad goodbye, we have new friends, memories and six bottles of dessert wine.

Then we drive over to see Lee and Rowan to meet their dogs. A retro caravan is parked in the drive and their home is full of stylish touches, colourful paintings on the wall, big coffee table books, neat cushions on sofas. The four of us sit out on their veranda drinking ice cold drinks in the shade while the drapes blow gently out of open windows. Their two little white Maltese terriers are equally as excited to meet us as Jayne is to meet them and they change laps frequently. Rowan's an artist and art teacher at the local college, we talk about travel, they want to take their caravan off, maybe across Australia. We talk about the pull of home, the pull of family and security on the one hand and travel, adventure and uncertainty on the other. They have grown up kids and grandchildren now too, probably more on the way at some point. Still, there's always the possibility they might take off with their caravan and go travelling. Lee and Rowan suggest that before we leave town they take us to see some sites and give the dogs a walk.

Gisborne's on the north shore of Poverty Bay. Famous for being the first landing place of James Cook's expedition in 1769, he called it Poverty Bay because he couldn't get the provisions he needed. We drive up to Kaiti Hill where you can see down to Cook's original landing spot. Then out to Makorori Beach, the dogs can run free on the miles of sandy shoreline, windswept, strewn with seaweed and driftwood. In the middle of the beach is the bent trunk of a whole tree, the wood worn white with the sea and the salty air. It's low tide and there's a long trail of solitary footprints in the sand near the water.

Time to make our own footprints, down to Hawke's Bay, also the place that Captain Cook sailed to after Poverty Bay. Around a hundred and fifty miles to Napier, for a gig at a gallery but there's been no publicity and only a couple of people show up. Then another at a winery, this one we're just background music, playing for people in the restaurant while they're eating. Someone says we should check out Te Mata Peak and see the views on our way out of town.

Te Mata Peak, a big mountain ridge that rises up out of a flat landscape, big enough for a road to take you right to the top. There's a car park and viewing platforms. We're high up, looking at the huge peak wrinkling in a line towards Hawke's Bay and the South Pacific. My eye naturally follows the ridge as it runs towards the sea until it falls away, folding back into the land long before the shoreline. You can see the towns of Havelock North and Hastings, Napier is twenty miles away and you can see that too. The coastline looks like a big bite size chunk has been eaten out of the side of the North Island.

Then we're heading south west down State Highway 2. A hundred miles to a gig at a cafe on the Manawatu River Gorge. Halfway there, just before the little town of Norsewood, the road passes over a small stream, it trickles under the road, insignificant, you'd never know it was there. By the time we get to the Manawatu River Gorge this stream has grown into the Manawatu River, over fifty metres wide where the Ballance Bridge crosses to take us to our cafe.

The generous hosting of the Kiwis has made us confident we'll be offered a place to stay tonight. We hope so, it's in the middle of nowhere. The cafe has a small veranda, just enough room to set up and play to the groups sat at picnic tables on the sloping lawn outside. People talking, eating and drinking beer. When we take a break a lady comes over and asks to buy a CD, would we mind signing it? She apologises that she can't stay for the second half.

At the end of the night we're packing up, it's getting dark, no offers of accommodation, it isn't that kind of gig. We ask the owner of the cafe, she suggests a campsite or holiday park. Too late for that really, no point in checking in to one at this time of night. As we're putting the gear in the back of the car one of the barmen comes out, says he'll ring his parents, see if they're okay with us stopping with them. We wait while he makes the call, we'll have to sleep in the car if nothing comes of this. I can hear his conversation, it's sounding positive. He ends the call, says no problem, his parents are happy to put us up, if we follow him in his car he'll take us past on his way home.

A small road bends up into the forest, pitch black, no chance of knowing where we're going without a guide, the road twisting and turning, snaking through the hills. We pull into the driveway of a log built house set in the woods. Then in through the front door, no one's there but the lights are on and there's music playing on a stereo somewhere on the ground floor. It sounds familiar, I recognise it but can't place it. What is it? Then I recognise it, it's our CD! The lady at the cafe that bought it and had to leave! Must be her, we only sold one. She appears from another part of the house,

"Hey, welcome, I'll show you your room."

In the morning we ask if we can take a shower,

"Sure you can, it's different but you might like it."

The bathroom's on the ground floor, I see straight away why she might've prepared us. Two of the bathroom's walls aren't there, it's completely open to the forest. There's a sink, a mirror and a free-standing bath, the shower cubicle has no screen, it's in the corner facing out into the woods. I can feel the outside air fresh and cool, circulating around me as I take my clothes off. The shower water's hot and high pressured, the trees nearly close enough to touch like I'm stood beneath a woodland waterfall, the steam rising up, drifting out through the branches and leaves above. It's the most beautiful shower experience I've ever had. I'm not a 'naked in the woods' kind of guy but if I'm ever in a position to design a house, I'll tell the builders not to bother with the outside bathroom walls, have some trees there instead.

State Highway 1 runs down the east coast to Wellington, the capital, the southernmost tip of the North Island. When we get to Otaki, even though the road is two miles inland we can see the sky over the sea is full of hundreds of different kites. We turn off the highway and drive to the beach, park up, then walk along the sand dunes. Kites, every size imaginable, not just diamond shaped kites trailing tails and streamers in the wind. The skies also full of super large inflatables, a huge spaceman, fantasy dragons, a teddy bear, whales and creatures from the ocean. A crazy troop of characters swimming together in an airborne stream of colour, like it's trying to make its way south down the coast while the strong headwind blows north, buoyantly holding them aloft.

Jayne's heard about an acoustic club that runs

one night a week on the same coast, a place called Kimbra's Lounge. We try to find out where it is on the map, probably some sort of cafe, bar or club but there's nothing that shows up and we can't locate it. This is New Zealand, the countries population is relatively small, nothing should be too hard to find.

Maybe that's what leads us to the answer, Kimbra's Lounge, it's in Kimbra's lounge, it's in her house. We ring the doorbell, Kimbra answers, a vibrant streak of red in her neat haircut, she's made up to see us. A lovely house too, beautiful artwork, the lounge all set with chairs in the round for anyone who wants to come along and play songs. The sitting room fills with regulars, everyone knows each other. Everyone takes it in turns to sing a song or play a piece of music, then sit back and listen, attentive as the focus moves around the room. Gary arrives late, a tall guy wearing a small floppy straw hat, he's brought lots of harmonicas. When it's our turn we ask him to play along to one of our songs and the room fills with a sound that sweeps and bends around the tune sewing the music together like a thread.

The ferry from the North Island to the South Island has a scheme for touring musicians. In exchange for playing a gig on board they give you a ticket for the crossing. First come first serve, you write to them with your preferred date and time, if it's free you've got your passage booked. The crossing takes around three hours and you play for about an hour in the bar area. Nobody checks on you or bothers you, no paperwork or bureaucracy, they trust you to do your job, they let you get on with it. There's a little stage and an announcement over the tannoy when you're about to start. A captive audience too, a ferry full of people with nothing to do and no other form of entertainment. That is until the boat sails the last leg of the journey through the Marlborough Sounds when everyone heads up on deck for the views.

We're packed up and finished by then and go up on deck to join them and marvel at the landscape. Sailing through a labyrinth of valleys half flooded by the sea, uninhabited forests covering it's rippling hills and peaks. Rolling contours of dark shadows and sunlit evergreens. Slow and steady until the small town of Picton appears on the shoreline, tucked into a deep inlet.

We've got a gig in Picton, it's just before we get the ferry back again in a couple of weeks. On the way out of town we stop in the high street, take a walk and put posters up in any shop that will have them.

First gig in the South Island is in Christchurch, down the west coast about two hundred miles from Picton. It's in a bar that does music nights, gigs and concerts. We've advertised it as much as we can in the local listings and sent posters in advance. Lovely little venue as it turns out, a small stage looking out over cosy little tables, nice lamps and lighting. We're all set but there's nobody here and this is a bar, no one's even coming in for a drink. We wait. Nothing.

After a while a couple come in with their dog and sit at one of the tables. We say hi, trying not to sound desperate, they're just here for a drink and didn't know anything about the music.

"Would you like to hear some?"

We play a few songs then go and join them at their table. Talk soon turns to the earthquake that devastated the city three years ago. They were here, it's still vivid to them, likely to stay that way. Back then they had two dogs, one of them died soon after, they're certain it was caused by the shock. The one that's with them today, it's fur turned white, they say it's not been the same dog since. We pack up our gear in silence, grateful that all we've had to endure is a no show gig.

Further down the west coast, another two hundred miles to Dunedin, a folk club gig, a spot on local radio too. An interview with Jeff, the friendly host of the breakfast show, he's invited us to stay with him and his partner Chanel. We get a message on the way, do we want to play a house concert for them as well? Yes we do, last minute gigs are rare, you grab them with both hands. Unbelievably, another one came in yesterday, another one of Jayne's sleepless nights where she discovered a hotel in the small town of Blackball that sometimes has music. They wrote back, said we can see who turns up, it's on our way back up in a few days time, we can stay the night there too.

We meet Jeff at the radio station. He's a smart casual kind of guy, suit jacket on top of a t-shirt, smooth head, beard and glasses. Dressed for business, and a rock concert. We chat on air to promote the gig at the folk club and once the show's finished we follow him home. He lives in the north of the city, not far from Baldwin Street, the world's steepest drivable street. We drive past it but don't go up, it looks dangerous, like a slope for a ski jump, plenty of parking on the roadside.

At Jeff's house tall windows look out on a lush green and well kept garden that wraps around the outside. Full of stylish things inside, the shelves in our bedroom are lined with an extensive CD collection. As we're placing our overnight bags on the bed Jeff puts his head round the door,

"Make yourself at home, I've got to pop out for a bit."

Jeff's in and out of the house through the day, car keys jangling in his hand. As well as hosting a radio show, he's a drummer in a band and a cat butler, looking after and feeding cats when owners are away. He makes sure they're okay, opens and closes curtains to give the house a lived in look, that's why he needs to keep going out.

Jeff and Chanel invite a group of friends over in the evening for our concert in their front room. They make food for everyone and people are kind and give donations. We go busking in Dunedin Market on the Saturday morning, then play the folk club on the Sunday night.

The shortest way to Invercargill, the southernmost city in the South Island, is to cut across inland from Dunedin. About a third of the way, at the small town of Balclutha, you get an option to come off the main road and take the scenic route through The Catlins. The Catlins, the name itself is enough to entice us in, sounds like somewhere in the Wild West, somewhere full of cowboys and canyons.

The road cuts through green, low lying hills, sheep farms, telegraph wires and telegraph poles running alongside us. An hour later and we're driving across a long narrow bridge that spans the wide mouth of a river. 'Welcome to Papatowai' says the first sign after the bridge, then a smaller sign further on in the shape of a surfboard, 'The Lost Gypsy, coffee and curios 700m'. Just a few houses at intervals along the roadside, a petrol pump attached to a small overground fuel tank outside a little general store. The road gently curves up the hill away from the river, I think we've just driven through Papatowai.

Round the corner of another bend and there's The Lost Gypsy on the right, the promise of coffee. A whale shaped mail box made of corrugated iron, a scarecrow holding a sign above it's head saying 'curios', a small area to park up. What is this place? We get out and stretch our legs. There's a much larger corrugated whale, this one suspended above a box with a wooden handle encouraging you to turn it. The whale starts to move when you do, the motion rolling through it's metal body from head to tail, creaking as it swims in the air.

Then through a wooden archway, 'the winding thoughts theatre of sorts' written across it, on the right a small silver coloured caravan, a young girl sat inside serving tea and coffee. On the left is a big green hippy bus in it's permanent resting place, the forest and foliage growing up around it. A staircase, half stone, half wood leads up to it's rear door, it's handrails made of oars from a rowing boat. Inside, the bus is a gallery full of gadgets, automated interactive gizmos, little signs everywhere, mottoes, musings, jokes, games you can play. There's a guy tinkering with one of the exhibits, we say hi. His name's Blair, it's his place, he's built everything, off grid and solar powered. He's been here since 1999, attracted by a simple life away from the city, no mortgage, a shelter and enough for food. He began collecting lost and found items, old and recycled objects, reworking them into interactive art, designs and installations that started to grow and spread out from the bus. The surf's good in Papatowai too.

After coffee we pay the $5 entrance fee and go through a gate at the back. An outdoor gallery extends along pathways in a rambling garden. Large rusty tentacles stick out of a hedge, like a giant metallic octopus is trapped inside. You turn a handle and the arms come to life and writhe around in the air. 'Rustic Automata' is what Blair calls it in an effort to give what he does a name, the vast creative array of recycled mechanical art on display everywhere.

Inside a covered circular hut is an upright piano, every key attached to a moving or sound making object round the room. Whistles, buzzes, door bells, whirring fans, alien noises, each key triggers something different.

We take a walk to the beach close by. Down a side street there's a roadside vegetable patch, a small piece of well tended ground abundant with edible produce. A neatly painted sign says 'Free Veggies, Help Yourself'. Then a short track that takes you to the shoreline, where the mouth of the river that we crossed on the long bridge meets the sea. The mouth is a bottleneck, the river's much wider before it gets to the ocean, pushing it's banks out into the forest, like it's hesitating, reluctant to leave the land and flow into the sea. The beach is windswept, rugged, rocky and weather beaten. Sand dunes full of jagged rocks, shells and driftwood. Strange seaweed, huge tangles of thick dark red rubbery ribbons, a dragon's portion of tomato pasta or giant bicycle inner tubes.

On the way out of Papatowai, at a give way sign, we let a large flock of sheep make their way across the road. Further on out of town there are three workmen in the road, all talking to each other. One of them has a Stop/Go sign, a red and green sided lollipop to show when it's safe to proceed. They pause to look at us, almost surprised, there's no other cars on the road, the guy with the sign keeps the red stop side pointed in our direction and waves us through.

In Invercargill we're the guests of Brad and

Chrissie. They run house concerts now and again for musicians passing through. Brad's tall, well over six foot and looks like Frank Zappa. He's a piano tuner and a musician, he and his wife play in a duo, they're a busy band playing weddings, ceilidhs, pubs and parties. The phone goes just after we arrive to see if they're free to play a function next weekend.

They have a big home, an open plan kitchen and lounge where they hold the concerts and invite friends and local music lovers along. One of their regulars likes to dance in front of the musicians during the gig, whatever the style of music, they ask if we mind. We say it doesn't happen enough.

You can't go to Invercargill without driving down to The Bluff, pretty much the southernmost tip of the South Island. A tourist destination, there's a well photographed sign post with distances and directions to various places around the world. London is 18,958km away. The other end of New Zealand, Cape Reinga, the tip of the North Island, where we were a few weeks ago is 1401km away.

Brad invites us to stay another night and in the evening we get the instruments out, they like to play all sorts of music and have a Celtic repertoire. They ask if we know 'Morrison's Jig'? Not only do we know it, our socks know it.

The only way is north now and we drive a couple of hours up to Arrowtown for a gig. Late summer is moving into autumn and the trees turning beautiful shades of red and gold. After Arrowtown it's a four hundred mile road trip north and up the west coast to Blackball for that last minute gig. What a road trip it is, skirting the edges of huge glassy lakes, passing through misty mountains, endless evergreen forests. Over bridges that cross wild rivers, the rapid water roaring through gorges, cascading over waterfalls. Only an occasional passing car or camper van, we've got the whole landscape to ourselves.

Blackball is small, just a couple of hundred residents but a rebellious history. We've got a gig at its one hotel and tavern, The Blackball Hilton, or as it should be known, 'Formerly The Blackball Hilton'. One of the chapters in the town's renegade past, it's just round the corner from Hilton Street and became 'The Blackball Hilton' in the 1990's. The international hotel chain heard of this little wooden two storey pub and boarding house and began legal proceedings against it for using the name. So, just like the musician Prince became 'The Artist Formerly Known As Prince', The Blackball Hilton became 'Formerly the Blackball Hilton'. Always punching above it's weight and another feather in it's rebel's cap. An attitude that goes back a hundred years when the local miners started a long strike that they eventually won and the campaign gave birth to the New Zealand Labour Party.

'Formerly The Blackball Hilton' have agreed to put us up for the night and give us breakfast, if there's any kind of turnout they'll pay us something too. We're playing in the bar area, the centre piece of the hotel, styled like an old English pub, a wooden bar with ageing bar stools, exposed beams across the ceiling with tankards hanging from them. There's a red baize pool table, an upright piano, a fire place. Behind the bar is a wall of photos, faded pictures of locals lifting their pint glasses, glazed eyes, red eyes, beers and cheers in the white light of a camera's flash. There are images of yesteryear too and postcards sent from around the world.

There's loud music on the stereo, the barman's friendly and offers us drinks. If it wasn't for the lines on his face he'd look young, long hair, a headband, wearing a black t-shirt, he bobs his head up and down to the music coming out of the speakers, a smile on his face most of the time. I'm not sure if he's smiling with us or at us. He likes rock music, particularly Guns'n'Roses. Says they've got a new music system in the bar and presses a key on an oversize laptop to play another song. The only thing is, he says, when you play a song you have to wait for it to play a few bars because it stops and you have to start it again. It plays through fine the second time, they haven't figured out how to fix it yet.

We set up in the window next to an old free-standing barrel used as a table. As we're putting up the mic stands the barman calls out,

"I'll turn the music off when you want to start."

A couple of locals turn up, it's low key, when the door to the bar opens everyone turns round to see who it is. Midweek, they say they often have bands play at the weekend, it can get quite raucous.

When we finish the barman offers us another drink. Before pouring it he goes over to the laptop, presses a key to start the song, his finger hovers over the keyboard, waiting. The song stops after the first few bars and he presses the key to get it going again. 'November Rain' by Guns'n'Roses, this time he's nodding through the slow piano and orchestral introduction, his upper body swaying to the music. As he's topping up our glasses I notice that the expression on his face has changed, his eyes now half closed and he's tensing his neck and shoulders. Focussed, he opens his mouth and I find out why, so he can sing along in the style of Axl Rose, raising the pitch of his voice up by constricting his throat and vocal chords but still keeping a gravelly edge to it. Singing along at full volume, word perfect, synchronised and looking me straight in the eye, he hands us our drinks.

9. SO MANY GOODBYES

"That tastes good."

We're at The Mussel Inn, two hours west of Nelson along the top of the South Island, sat at a handmade timber table in a converted wool shed, all natural wood, there are artefacts and instruments on the walls. Jayne's taken her first sip of Captain Cooker, the most popular beer, the one they recommended she try first. Our table's in front of the purpose built stage, there's a high end sound system, the mixing desk's built into a wooden table at the other end of the bar.

The Mussel Inn is in the middle of nowhere and not on the way to anywhere either. Even though we've taken the road here, over the mountains, skirting the edges of the Abel Tasman National Park, we'll turn around and take the same road back. We've been told it's a definite destination on any musician's tour of New Zealand.

"When you've finished your drink I'll show you where you're staying."

Andrew's a tall, gentle mannered guy, him

and his wife Jane built The Mussel Inn, built it themselves. They also built their home, where we're staying tonight, a two storey log house at the end of a path that leads from the back of the venue. Andrew says the musicians always stay with them, we're in one of the guest bedrooms upstairs. As I'm climbing the stairs my hand reaches out to feel the walls, the huge logs stacked lengthways on top of each other, the natural and untreated wood, the texture and grain still visible. It's so solid, Andrew says it should last 300 years or more. Then he leaves us to it, he has things to do, all the beer's brewed on site too. The house is quiet but it feels alive, it feels like I need to speak in a whisper,

Back in the bar, Andrew comes to sit with us, he's been checking in at the brewery, then the orchard and vegetable garden before he does our soundcheck. They've been brewing Captain Cooker here for twenty years, inspired by New Zealand's first ever beer. Made in 1773 on the South Island by Captain James Cook, brewed as a remedy for scurvy and flavoured with Manuka leaves. The Mussel Inn use water from a stream in the hills, the beer gets it's name from the pigs that Captain Cook released onto the South Island. Released so they'd breed in the wilderness and provide food for men on future trips, they became known as Captain Cookers. The offspring of these wild pigs are still out in the bush today.

After the gig, the next morning, there's an everyday ritual, coffee and freshly made muffins on the deck for the team of staff who work here. Andrew and Jane stay standing and aren't around long, we go and try to find them to say thanks and goodbye. Jane's upstairs in the office, replying to the countless emails she gets every day from musicians who want to play here,

"Thanks for the music," she says, and she really means it.

Andrew is out in the orchard harvesting hops they've started growing, he thanks us for the music too. As we drive out we head the wrong way and need to turn around, a little further up the highway there's a side road, we pull in next to a blue street sign on top of a pole that says 'Excellent Street'.

When we lived in Hastings we used to go to a great cafe run by a young Kiwi woman. It was a while before we realised she'd taken over the cafe. We'd gone in once before, hungry and looking for a menu, the previous owner had confronted me,

"What can I do for you?"

"Maybe a sandwich, what have you got?"

"What kind would you like?"

I wasn't sure,

"What kind of things do you do?"

"What kind of things do you like?"

The door to the street seemed to move further away, we negotiated our way to some sort of a sandwich.

Things couldn't have been more different when Jae took it over. Busy all day, every day, home made specials, fresh sandwiches and cakes, all served with a smile, a big smile. One of the things you notice most about Jae, a big toothy beam beneath her neat bob haircut. So it wasn't long before Jayne and I were going there regularly for lunch and she became a friend.

Now she's come back to New Zealand, her and her new partner came back last year to settle in Nelson, at the top of the South Island. They've invited us to stay when we play our first gig in town. A house in the suburbs where the road rises up into the hills, detached houses, balconies, short sloping driveways.

Jae's got her apron on when we arrive, the oven light is on and the warm aroma of something tasty in the air, the kitchen cleaned down and tidy. When we sit down to eat it tastes as good as we remember. Early days for them here, they've not been back long. Jae's working at a cafe, at the Wearable Art Museum, she says it's a pretty cool place, we should check it out before we leave. Her partner Rob's a hairdresser, he's taken a job at a salon until he can maybe start one of his own. They're going to make it work here, they're committed to it, he's shipping over his VW camper van from England, he calls it The Colonel. They've bought paddle boards, the big ones you stand up on and row along the river or out to sea on a calm day.

Our first gig is at The Boathouse, a harbour

venue built over the water a hundred years ago by the local rowing club. A large one room club house, cabaret tables around a high stage in the middle of the longest wall. A proper venue, ticketed entry, Jae and Rob come along and join a small crowd who've come to sit in candlelight and watch our show.

The next day before we leave we take Jae's advice and drive out to the Wearable Art Museum. She's in the cafe, in her work apron and takes a break to get us into the exhibition. Black studio spaces with atmospheric lighting, a gallery of mannequins wearing fine art, clothing tailored for strange dreams or bizarre nightmares. Fashion on a dark and surreal trip. Some designs are outlandish, others very simple. Alongside a fantasy Elizabethan costume is a dress made entirely of the little coloured tags that loaves of bread are sealed with. All the square plastic pieces neatly held together with tiny gold rings like chain mail, the best before dates still readable on each one.

We go back to the cafe, Jae doesn't like goodbyes and says we have to agree not to say any. Her smile has faded, no farewells she says again. We all know it'll be a long time until we see each other again. She takes a breath, says to look around the museum as long as we want.

Then we drive over to the other side of Nelson, to stay with Anna and Pete, they run an acoustic club in town and can put us up. Another hilltop suburb of Nelson, the road steeper, past bungalows that sit behind overgrown hedges and trees. We pull up and park on the small road alongside theirs, the one with a metal roof, more exposed at the top, views of the mountains all around the city.

Anna welcomes us, Pete's working in the garage but comes in a little while later when he realises we've arrived. Their bungalow is compact, we drink tea in the lounge, at a small table tucked behind two armchairs that face out of the main window. Talk turns to music, songs and then instruments. They go into the next room and bring back two heavy black cases, their prize possessions, a couple of high end guitars. Pete lets me try one, the wood is resonant, the strings sing beneath my fingers, the sound is three dimensional.

I hand it back to him then sit on the floor, Jayne takes an armchair, Anna and Pete play us a song. I can see the hills of Nelson in the distance through the window. Pete has a voice that's strong and warm, lived in. The song is by Steve Earle, about a guy who feels a bond with eagles, lives high up in the mountains. 'Me and The Eagle', a big sky song, lonely, riding a horse way up above the timberline. They finish and we ask for another, they play 'Killing the Blues'. I've heard the song many times before but not like this, they draw out something more, something sadder. The lyrics elusive, emotional, enigmatic, Jayne and I are both transfixed, blown away. Pete and Anna don't believe us when we tell them, they think we're being polite guests. No good trying to persuade Pete how good we thought that was, he's a man of few words, he goes back out to do some more work in the garage.

We've nearly circled the South Island. One gig left to close the loop, not counting the one on the ferry in exchange for our ticket. So we're back where we started, in the small harbour town of Picton, we'd put posters up in some shops in town when we got off the ferry a few weeks ago. The gig's at a restaurant on the waterfront next to green grass, palm trees and a marina with expensive looking boats. You can see the whole bay, the ferry coming in, the hills and mountains wrapped around it.

The restaurant's run by Peter, a Swiss guy, the trace of a German accent when he speaks. He likes to help out touring musicians but it's midweek, he says he's not sure how many will come along. We set up our gear and Peter gets the kitchen to make us a meal, a storm is picking up outside, there's only a couple of diners in tonight. One of Peter's friends comes in and the two of them sit at a table together to watch. After the gig he says he'll get us some accommodation and takes us to a backpackers hostel up the road and pays for our room.

Next morning the weather's got worse. Strong winds as we drive to the ferry, heavy rain lashing down. The windscreen wipers working overtime to keep some visibility, but there's no rush, the ferry's delayed. Departure times are moving further and further back, each crossing is taking longer, the rolling on and rolling off much slower. We'll be here a while.

We do a crossword. A member of staff comes down the queue of cars to give an update, he's leaning into the wind, one hand holding his hood on. Jayne edges the top of the window down, the wind howls through the gap, rain splashes into the inside of the door. When he hears about our gig on board we get a pass that says 'Easy Access' so we can get on first and he waves us to another queue. He says it'll be a while yet.

I pull out some paper, suggest we do some creative writing, just write three pages of A4 without pausing. Most of what gets written on the page is rubbish, my hand repeating words and phrases just to keep the momentum going without stopping. One phrase stands out when I read it back, 'the captain and me', written forwards and then backwards just to keep writing. We work on the idea,

Blood on the foredeck, tears in the sea
A storm on the waters of Galilee
We sailed from the island, we sailed to be free
Me and the Captain, the Captain and me

Tired of life, a slave to the task
We took all our colours down from the mast
Burning bridges recklessly
Me and the Captain, the Captain and me

We split the shore, breaking the tide
A howling wind kept the spirits alive
He was a father and brother was he

Me and the Captain, the Captain and me

Down, down, the warnings we found
All for the light, or we'll come aground
We kept the watch continuously
Me and the Captain, the Captain and me

I was despair, in doubt constantly
He was calm moving silently
Onward our journey, endlessly
Me and the Captain, the Captain and me

With tears on the foredeck, blood in the sea
A storm on the waters of Galilee
We sailed on the ocean, we sailed to be free
Me and the Captain, the Captain and me

The crossing over to the North Island is choppy, the ferry lurching up and down. We can't stand up to play, not today, even sitting down there's balancing to do. Abrupt shifts from heavy gravity to weightlessness, dips and swells. The microphone swings away, every time it does Jayne has to stop playing to retrieve it and swing it back. The passengers are in a good mood, we're finally sailing after hours of waiting around. We have a captive audience, all the chairs in the lounge are full, everyone's grateful of entertainment, nobodies outside looking at the view.

By the time the boat arrives back in Wellington the storm has calmed down, everything's quieter, just large puddles of muddy rain water everywhere. Windswept, but this is 'Windy Wellington', a contender for the world's windiest city. Making our way back north now, the last leg of the trip. We have some good friends in The Bay of Plenty, Kat and Mat, there's a gig we're playing just up the road from them. Friends from when we lived in our bedsit in Brighton, ten years or so ago, before they emigrated here and we moved to Hastings.

You'd say we were best friends by the amount of time we used to hang out together. Long weekends at their house, sitting round their kitchen table or in their back yard in the summer. Their two boys were very young then, toys and playthings scattered around the floor, reusable nappies hanging on the washing line. Mina the dog, she always had an eye open for the fallout of food from the kid's bowls, always bound to be something making it's way to the floor, pasta, bits of carrot or broccoli that drop or get thrown from the high chair. Mina's a good dog, a street dog from Perpignan in France, a mix of breeds, the look of a lean short haired German Shepard. Well behaved, never any trouble, like she knew how lucky she was, waiting patiently for us to take her for a walk up to Brighton Racecourse. The extended preparations that had to be made to get a family with young children out of the house. Rucksacks with important things in, socks and shoes to find, laces to tie, little arms to put through the sleeves of jackets. She'd wait quietly through it all.

As we pull off the state highway and up the

track to their house Mina comes to greet us, I like to think she knows who we are. Not moving so quick these days, her hair going grey but all the more lovely for it. Her mum and dad aren't going grey though. Kat with her long jet black hair, tanned skin, Mat's boyish happy face, they still look as young as they ever did, excited to show us around. Mina keeps close, hugging the sides of our legs as we walk through the orchard of avocado trees at the back of their house. We've come in the right season, they're ripening all the time, the trees are full of them. There's a tree house built into the branches of one of the larger ones. Mat's carpentry skills, he's built a workshop on site too.

Kat has a couple of horses, down the hill at the front they've built a dressage arena. Out by one of the fences is Barney, their rescued pet sheep, he wanders anywhere he likes. Kat gets out the hair clippers now and again to trim him down, sheer off his shaggy wool in the hot weather. She used to do the same for me, Mat and Jayne in their kitchen in Brighton, she's not a hairdresser, she's just not afraid to wield a pair of scissors. Not afraid to take on any task, rolling up her sleeves and getting it done, the same attitude to anything like mucking out horses or making a meal. Kat's still serving up her one pot signature dish, 'Pasta Avo', the meal that we ate at their kitchen table back in England all those years ago. The difference is that now the avocados come from the trees in their garden. It's taken time to find their feet here but they're thriving now, property, land and a lifestyle they could never afford in England.

Kat and Mat come out to the gig and we have to say goodbye to them there, at the end of the night. The adrenaline of the show masks a sad farewell, we say we'll be back soon but really we don't know when that'll be.

The road signs are all pointing back to Auckland but there's one more reason to ignore them, a venue off the beaten track, at the top end of what the Kiwi's call the Forgotten World Highway. A little theatre in the small town of Taumarunui, in King Country, a big rural area west of the centre of the North Island. Jayne got the gig some time ago but we've had no contact since she booked it, we sent a few posters but haven't heard anything.

The town is built around a main street, a few shops down one side of the road. We pull up in the afternoon and park outside the small wooden one storey theatre. The side door is open so we go in, a group of children are rehearsing a musical. We ask an adult if there's anyone who knows about this evening's concert but they don't know anything, they'll be finishing soon and locking up. We take a walk down the high street, maybe we'll see one of our posters advertising the concert tonight. There's a sports bar, another store selling meat and veg, we can't see any posters. One shop has a notice saying 'no gangs'. At a public phone box we call the contact number on the email but there's just an answerphone.

Back at the theatre, we're parked right outside, the plain white washed wooden front gives nothing away, no billboards, noticeboards or indication of what's on. Why didn't we check in a few days ago? Why didn't we make sure everything was okay, firm it up beforehand? Is the show on, even if it is, is anyone going to come along?

We walk up the high street again looking harder for a poster, a sign that we're playing tonight, that someone, somewhere knows it's on, still nothing. Then back to the car again, the notion of turning the key in the ignition, taking off and leaving town comes up, we talk ourselves out of it.

The kids who've been rehearsing start leaving the theatre, then the adults, the last one locks the door behind him. We stand on the pavement looking up and down the street, nobody around.

A car comes along the road, pulls up beside ours, a woman rolls down the window,

"Hi, did you guys try to ring me?"

She opens the side door and we take our gear in, through to the auditorium and the stage, plush red curtains, a black backdrop, rows of tiered seating,

"We've sold quite a few tickets."

We soundcheck and the theatre starts to fill up with an audience. A full house, everyone's in a happy mood, lively, lots of applause. In the interval we go out to the foyer and talk to people, sell CD's, sign them like proper celebrities. We get talking to a lady from the audience and mention that we weren't sure if anyone would be there to see us. She says she made a point to tell everyone they had to come along. We thank her, she says she didn't want it to be another event everyone missed because they didn't know it was on.

Then we drive back up to Auckland, more goodbyes. Goodbye to Gillian and Arthur and Bob the dog. A final goodbye gig, Sunday afternoon at a folk club, Rick and some other friends from Auckland say they'll come along. The club is right by a flyover that crosses the motorways going in and out of the city. We're early and take a walk over the bridge, looking down on the big spaghetti network of traffic being pumped in, around and out of Auckland. Relentless, restless movement, always going somewhere else.

After the gig, as we're leaving, just about to pull away, some young people get into the car parked in front of ours. Their reverse lights go on and they back straight into us, a loud solid metal clunk. Damn, we've had the car all this time, our last day too. We get out and inspect the damage, there's a dent in the front number plate, we exchange numbers.

At the car rental at the airport we hand the keys back and the guy with the clipboard goes round the outside, checking it over. We show him the number plate and say we have the details of the people who backed into us yesterday. He shrugs, it doesn't matter he says, and adds another little cross to the sheet.

10. ON THE WALTZ

There's nothing like playing a noisy English pub to wake yourself up and shake off jet-lag. The loud laughter, the kind that only occurs in places serving large amounts of alcohol, people don't laugh like that when they're at home. My body clock hasn't a clue what the time is. It's a Thursday night, at least it's not the weekend when there's even more reasons for people to shout across the bar.

We'd picked the van up yesterday from the street in Hastings where we left it. Everything was okay, just a deflated front tyre that didn't take long to pump up and then we were on our way. Familiar signs that we're back on the road in England again, things that amuse us, lay-bys with vans selling 'hot and cold food', the unappetising reference to temperature. Then the signs at the outskirts of towns saying 'historic market town'. A market town, wasn't every town once a market town with a few new town exceptions?

After tonight we're taking the ferry from Dover, onto a busking festival in Germany, not far from Stuttgart. The only thing is, there's a big hole in the diary, a big chunk of time after it, about a month before we've got anything else. We got accepted for the festival, said yes, then researched gigs to tie in with it but never got any responses. Cafes, pubs, bars, there are loads of places in Germany that have live music but we couldn't get a reply from any of them. We're going to need to go busking in between, quite a bit, but we've heard Germany is difficult for street music, particularly if you use a small amplifier, it's likely we'll get stopped but we've never tried.

Driving down to the festival we decide to give it a go on the way, somewhere not too obvious. Big, well known places aren't worth trying anyway, too much of an operation driving into a big city, finding parking then getting into the centre. Plus in the big cities they've seen it all before, unless you're setting fire to yourself and doing backflips you go unnoticed. You're just tiny fish in a huge sea, swimming against the tide. I'm studying the map on the phone, making sure we find a town that's big enough to be busy, zooming in to check it's got a pedestrian area. It's all very random, total guesswork. Then there's all the other factors like the weather, roadworks, special events, other buskers and the possibility that the police might decide to stop us. Let's just put those things out of our mind, turn up and see what happens.

I pick Ludwigshafen, a town on the Rhine, the opposite side of the river to Mannheim. Parking's easy, in a cinema and bowling complex not far from the centre. We walk in, there's a long pedestrian street but it's not clear which end is more central. I go to ask a man walking by but he briskly waves me away, brushing me off, why would he do that? I keep thinking about it, then I see someone sleeping in a doorway, the man must've thought I was begging.

Down one end is the entrance to an indoor shopping centre, people flowing in and out of the multiple doors. We pitch up on the opposite corner, not everyone will be coming this way but most of them will. There's a couple of benches opposite, the sun's shining on them.

We start to play, people take a pause on the benches, listen to a few songs then come over and drop some change and move on. Sometimes mothers sit with their young children, sending them over with a coin. A precarious little trip for smaller ones, their tiny hand gripped tightly around the money, looking back over their shoulder for reassurance as they get closer. We smile, try to look approachable, try to forget the time a child fell into the guitar case and burst into tears.

A well dressed mature gentleman in a suit comes up to us. We hadn't seen him, we're normally aware of who's around, who's listening and watching, somehow he's gone unnoticed. His name's Klaus, we shake hands and say a proper hello, his English is very good. He works for a bank and is on his lunch break, he's been sat on a bench further along, says he's a big fan of acoustic music. Last year the town had an acoustic music festival, he was disappointed, the music didn't live up to any of his expectations. Our music was the kind of thing he was looking for. Would we like to play a concert at his house? How much would we charge? We take his email address, we tell him that we're on the way to a festival and we'll get in touch in the next few days to arrange things. Maybe one of the artists at the festival will have an idea what to charge for a concert around here.

The festival's set inside the grounds of a big estate, a grand stately home kind of place surrounded by large parklands, woods and open spaces. The whole thing is sponsored by a major bank, their logo and brand prominent on the posters. A minibus brings all the street acts in from a youth hostel a couple of miles away. Some acts set up straight away on a central walkway before anything official's even started, putting in extra time to make extra money.

There's an act attracting a big crowd, every time we pass I'm drawn over to stand with the audience, watching and listening to them, two guys with electric guitars. One of the guitars looks very different, a half teardrop shaped body that runs the length of the neck, only three strings, some extra long frets, it looks medieval. They have a lot of equipment, lots of effects and they build up loops and play hypnotic riffs and solos over the top. The whole thing is mesmerising, I find it hard to move on, music swirling and building into a trance like the next layer will bring me salvation. I ask a German street performer standing next to me in the crowd,

"Who are these guys?"

"'The Famous Unknowns', busking legends."

The festival calls itself a busking festival. On the one hand it is, on the other it isn't. There are small stages around the grounds and each act gets slots in various locations. After each performance they say you can collect money from the crowd, but it's a raised stage you're playing on, not a street, the dynamics are different, there's also an entrance fee to the event and everyone's paid to get in already.

Back at the youth hostel, there's a strict time for breakfast, the shutters come down and everything's cleared away by 10am. We're sat in the canteen in the late morning, talking to a few of the other acts when The Famous Unknowns come in. They look tired but not like they've just got up. The manager, usually straight faced, is all smiles and handshakes with them, he goes to the kitchen, brings out some breakfast which they eat like they haven't had food for days.

When their pace of eating has slowed down I go over and complement them on their sound. They're tired and hungry, they've been in Stuttgart busking all morning. I apologise and volunteer to leave them alone but they come around and warm up to a conversation. Lindsay's Australian, wears a big black Russian peaked military cap, he looks like Robin Williams. Carlos is taller and from

The Netherlands. They've been busking and street performing for years, for decades, they used to play in Leicester Square in London back when you were allowed to, when the rate of exchange was good,

"I've also been at the other end, stood on a street for three hours and earned 50p."

Lindsay's talking, they're both still devouring their way through breakfast. I'm fascinated by the instrument that he plays. He tells me it's an Appalachian dulcimer that he's hand built and fitted with a pickup to use like a synthesiser. He busks on his own in Australia in the winter, flies over to Europe for the summer. Carlos lives in Amsterdam, as a resident he can get permits to play on the streets there, thirty minute slots. I figure I've taken enough of their time, they could probably use a rest, Carlos says they're going to finish eating and get to the festival early for a good spot.

At one of the stages we join forces with an Italian klezmer act, we both help each other out by collecting money at the end of each of our shows, much easier to ask for donations on behalf of someone else. There's a voting system at each stage too, a box to collect votes for the audience's favourite acts of the festival. The top three get a bonus payment at the end of the weekend, quite a sizeable sum. When I go to the office at the end of the last day for our expenses I can see the unopened boxes of votes. It's all rigged. They're announcing the winners on the main stage before all the boxes have even been collected.

◆ ◆ ◆

We write to Klaus about a date for his house concert and agree on the following Sunday. All we have to do is keep ourselves busy for a week, see if we can earn something in the meantime. If the Famous Unknowns went busking in Stuttgart then let's try there first. They use an amplifier, maybe we'll be allowed to use ours. We get up at 5am, drive into the city early to avoid the rush hour and morning traffic. Once we're parked we get in the back and sleep for a couple of hours until the shops open.

The city streets are still quiet when we start, a trickle of people making their way through town. After playing for ten minutes a policeman comes along. A congenial guy, small, wide around the waist, only speaks a little English. Looking at us and our instruments he smiles and points, first at the guitar,

"Yes," he says. Then he points at the ukulele,

"Yes," he says again. Then he points at the amplifier,

"No."

Amplifiers are not allowed on the streets of Stuttgart. I want to tell him the Famous Unknowns were here just a few days ago but instead we pack up and leave.

We try various other towns and cities over the next few days, every time it's the same. Even before we've set up sometimes and always within ten minutes, a policeman comes along, shakes his head and moves us on. By Thursday we give up trying, we'll just wait for Klaus's house concert at the weekend. After that we need a plan for the three and a half weeks between now and the next festival in Austria. What to do? We remember talking to our friend Paulo, the one man band from Italy, him telling us about Denmark. How he'd played all around the country, mostly didn't have any problems. That's it, we'll go there, we'll be earlier than when their summer holidays start but anything's got to be better than our attempts here.

Klaus wants us to play in his garden and invites a handful of people, mostly his family and a couple of friends. His wife has a wide-eyed look when she's speaking to us, tolerating her husband's impromptu arrangement with strangers he met on the street and the party she's having to cater for. They're having another get together tomorrow too, Germany's first game in the football World Cup. Everyone is very kind to us, we sit round a big table outside and eat a meal together before the concert on their neat and tidy back lawn.

Afterwards we set off north, to Denmark. Five hundred miles, the A7 motorway all the way, almost a straight line slicing right up the middle of Germany. Up to Jutland, the part of Denmark that sits on top of northern Germany like a stove pipe hat. It's not until the end of the next day that we get there, the roads quieter the closer we get to the border. We'll start busking tomorrow.

The first town is Aabenraa, not far from the border. I check out the population, around 16,000, that's quite small. Maybe we'll use it as a warm up, see what happens. We walk in through pretty little streets, buildings painted cornflour blue, light grey, apricot, all with white windows, little counting houses and cottages.

There's a pedestrian street in the middle of town, a walkway paved with bricks in a herringbone pattern. It runs the length of the town centre, little shops and boutiques along both sides. We set up in a space near a toy shop. It's very quiet, Paulo told us he came here during the Danish summer holidays, we're about ten days away from them starting. Still, we get some change thrown in the case, we want to take a look at this strange new currency we're collecting but have to wait. You can't bend down on the street and stare at the money, it doesn't look good.

We change location after an hour, just in case someone somewhere is taking offence. Further along we play near a cafe, two ladies come up and want to buy a CD, we have no idea how much to charge. We explain we've just arrived in Denmark, ask them what they normally pay, trying not to sound like we're haggling or don't have a clue what we're doing. Best go for a round number, we agree on 100 Danish Krone, around £10 sterling, and get a note from each of them. Crisp sepia coloured bank notes, proper paper money, our first day, our first earnings. It really is too quiet though, tomorrow we need somewhere bigger.

The next day and the next town up the east coast is Haderslev, population around 21,000. That won't be much different, we drive straight past and up to the next, Kolding, population more like 60,000, that should be better. We park up and have a look. It's still quiet, just a small number of people walking the streets, you could count them on one hand. No different to yesterday. Maybe we'll have to go to much bigger places and everything will get busier at the weekend or when the summer holidays start.

Esbjerg is a town on the west coast, until recently they ran a ferry service to England from there. The biggest town we've been to so far, the main pedestrian street is much wider and longer, the shops are much bigger. Definitely more people which shows in the amount of Danish coins getting thrown in the case. We're learning to tell them apart. The best ones are the big gold ones, twenty kroner, worth over £2, weighty and substantial, kroner written in capital letters that look ancient and regal. The other gold coin is the ten kroner, smaller, around the size of a one pound coin. Then there's the big silver coin with a hole in the middle, the five kroner, we get some euros thrown in the case as well. A bit of Norwegian and Swedish change too, whether we'll ever be able to spend these other currencies is another matter.

A couple sit and watch us from a bench. They eventually come over, encouraging each other.

She has a smiling round and red cheeked face, short cropped blonde hair, her name's Susann, her husband's name is Klaus. Another Klaus, it seems irrelevant to mention the coincidence. Anyway she's got something to say and is trying to find the words to say it. Her English is basic, his even more so, he backs up everything Susann says by nodding and the pieces start to fit together.

They're going to a friend's wedding tomorrow and would like us to play a few songs. It will be their gift to the bride and groom as they've yet to buy them a present, it'll be a surprise. The groom is a *Wandergesellen*, Susann can't translate the word and we don't understand the explanation. Anyway, can we do it, how much would we charge to play a short set? Everyone says stick a nought on anything to do with a wedding but this is just a few songs, these guys don't look wealthy, it's not their wedding either, it's just their gift for the couple. We ask for an equivalent of our recent house concert, house concerts are becoming Klaus concerts! They look disappointed, you can tell we've asked for too much and they can't afford it. The proposition sounds too interesting to miss out on, it's tomorrow, we agree on a thousand kroner, around £100.

It's in a nearby town, we exchange phone numbers. As it's a surprise, she's going to text us after they've had the sit down meal in the early evening. She'll announce it to the wedding guests, say a few words, then we'll go in, set up and play.

The next morning we decide to stay in

Esbjerg, the wedding is only twenty miles away, we'll busk first then make our way over. It's Saturday, town is much busier but a few minutes in and a policeman stops us, says we need a licence, we can get one from the police station or the tourist information office. Maybe we'll do that another time, we leave it for the day and head over to be nearer the wedding, count ourselves lucky we have an actual gig.

Susann texts us an update in the early evening, the meal is delayed, we need to wait. An hour later she messages again that it could be happening soon, we drive to the venue, a kind of community building with a large hall. Standing in the corridor we can see through the glass doors, everyone sat at big round tables, pink tablecloths. A lot of the men are dressed in black velvet costumes, fitted black waistcoats with large cream coloured buttons, white collarless shirts and bell bottom trousers. Most have got top hats on but there are other shapes and sizes too, fedoras, peaked hats, some with very wide brims. They look like stylish Victorian chimney sweeps. The wedding meal has finished, people are sat back away from the tables.

Klaus and Susann come out to the corridor to say hello, she says now we're here she's going to announce us, Klaus nods. She seems nervous, so are we, but we act like we do this all the time, turn up and play music uninvited and unexpected at a wedding. They go back in and resume their place at the table. Then we see Susann stand up, clink the side of her glass with a teaspoon, signalling she wants to make a speech. She starts talking in Danish to the wedding guests, we haven't a clue what she's saying, it probably isn't,

"Well, we were shopping yesterday and saw this couple busking and thought you might like to hear them."

Maybe it is. We step through the glass door, all heads turn to look at us, a room full of wedding guest's eyes. The big day. I feel the weight of responsibility get heavier, not only for the occasion but also for the friendship that might be hanging by a thread between Susann and Klaus and the bride and groom.

Perhaps it's the celebratory mood in the air, the grand sense of a special day or just a large consumption of alcohol but everybody's up for it. Some guests get up to dance and at the end of each song there's the sound of whooping applause. After half an hour we count ourselves lucky we've got away with it and finish, the crowd are shouting,

"Extra number, extra number."

The Danish way of asking for an encore! We shake hands with Klaus and Susann, all smiles and happy red faces, they introduce us to the bride and groom, they say their wedding gift was a nice surprise.

A small group of the guys in costume are smoking outside, cigarettes in one hand, beer bottles in the other. They're English is good, they're craftsmen, mostly carpenters following a long tradition that goes back centuries. *Wandergesellen* from Germany, journeymen, same as the groom, the bride is Danish. They say they're on the waltz, wandering away from home for three years and a day. Taking work to improve their craft, apprenticing themselves on the way. With five euros in their pocket at the start, they return home with the same amount to show they've only worked for the experience.

Klaus and Susann come out as we're loading the car and give us a 1000 Kroner note. I tuck it safely into our money belt, this one bill worth over a hundred pounds. It's gone ten o'clock but the sky is still light, we say goodbye and that we'll stay in touch and hope to see them again sometime. There's a car park in town for camper vans, the sun setting as we join the others who've pulled in for the night.

The long days are coming to their peak, June, one year on the road. Summer's just beginning and that only means one thing, the steady decline of daylight hours from now on. Makes us conscious of where they lead, to winter, months away but last year we just let things roll too much, left it too late, left it too much to chance. Jayne's been keeping her eye on house sits again, something that'll see us through the coldest part of the year.

There's an email in her inbox, about one in Ireland, for three months, can she give the woman a call? Her name's Dervla, she lives in County Waterford. Jayne rings, puts the phone on loud speaker so I can listen in. Dervla's in her eighties, she's a writer, she's going to the Middle East to finish a book and needs a pet sitter. Her home's a set of separate buildings around a courtyard, in the winter she spends most of her time in one of them, the one with the log burner. She says some of her friends find it cold, one of them came to stay and never took her coat off the whole time she was there. Dervla's direct, tells it like it is, she's charming too and Jayne can't help but say yes, we'll do it. Maybe it's her Irish charm, the sound of her adventurous spirit, or the summer sunshine streaming through our window at the moment that's telling us it's going to be okay. If she's in her eighties and she's alright there in the winter it must be fine. After the call we look her up, Dervla Murphy, she cycled from Ireland to India in 1963, wrote a book about it called *Full Tilt*.

Time to get on and fill our purse with money for the winter. We go across to the east of Jutland again, picking any town with a reasonable sized population. In Horsens we set up on the main street in the centre of town opposite a group of benches, a nice wide pedestrian walkway. An old guy comes by on a bicycle as we're getting ready, he stops in front of us, says hello. His white hair's ruffled, clothes a little rumpled, he introduces himself as Stephan,

"How are you doing today Stephan?"

He shifts his weight to get comfortable on the saddle,

"Well," he says, matter of factly, taking his time,

"When I woke up this morning I wasn't

feeling so good but after my medication and a couple of beers I began to feel a little better."

He's happy seeing us here, playing music in town, he loves music, he used to play in a duo with his brother. Stephan pauses, says his brother passed away not long ago, his eyes go somewhere else for a moment, he steadies the front wheel of the bike. Then he says they played all over Germany and Denmark for many years, good years, he was lucky and glad he did it. With one hand back on the handlebars he says he hopes we have good luck today. Stephan cycles away, his free hand waving a slow goodbye all the way down the street.

We try the big city of Aarhus a few times with varying degrees of luck. There's plenty of places to play but there are other buskers too and the city crowds have seen it all before. Still, you never know who's listening. The big shopping streets have offices on the upper floors, a dentist gives us a 50 Kroner note in his lunch break and says he, his staff and patients have been enjoying the music all morning through their open window on the top floor.

There's a big harbour in Aarhus, with a lot of construction going on, modern apartment blocks in different stages of completion, state of the art aspirational accommodation, contemporary angular architecture. In the middle of it all is the clubhouse for the sailing club, a remnant of a bygone era when the only things here were boats moored along jetties. Now it's sitting in the midst of a tidal wave of urbanisation.

The sailing club allow camper vans to stay on the small gravel car park at one end of the long waterfront. We park up and walk along the quayside to the clubhouse, it's only £10 a night to stay and you get a code to access the showers. We put the money in one of the envelopes in a box inside the front door. There's a drinks machine for members inside, cheap, especially for Denmark. It takes coins so we offload the smaller denominations we've collected.

On the bed in the back of the van we sit and look out at the boats on the marina. With the side door's slightly open on the sheltered side, there's the sound of the wind as it blows through the masts and the rigging, whistling, singing a never ending song. Right behind us are some modern apartment blocks, these ones finished, the occasional silhouette of a resident when they move around, the blue light of a TV screen flickering on the wall. Behind the apartment block are tall cranes and the next phase of dockland construction.

A woman in a red sailing jacket and a head scarf comes round on a bicycle and says a cheery hi. She's the harbour master this week, her turn to do the duties, her and her husband live on one of the boats. No other camper vans tonight, just us, parked amongst some cars. I tell her we might stay a couple more nights. When she finds out we're musicians she whispers to us that we don't have to put any more money in the box and cycles off.

On a sleepy Sunday after Aarhus we follow our nose down the coast, south of the city, no towns to speak of but we're not looking for anything in particular. Maybe a picnic spot by the sea, somewhere out of the way. We come across one, next to a solitary restaurant in the middle of nowhere. A car park with high hedges all around, on the other side are picnic tables nestled into the hedge like booths in a cafe, a strip of wild grassland along a low cliff edge.

Nobody's here, just swallows swooping back and forth over the long grass while we cook up a meal, silent except for the sound of a gentle breeze and the hiss of the stove. After we've eaten, as I'm boiling water for some coffee, Jayne pulls a business card out of her pocket,

"Back in a minute."

She goes round to the restaurant but comes straight back, the owner was busy, she just left him the card. Five minutes later, our coffee cups still warm in our hands and she gets an email from him asking what we'd charge for playing. Two emails later and we've settled on a price, a date in ten days time and they'll give us a meal and some drinks. The restaurant is Himmel og Hav, Heaven and Sea.

Over a bridge from Jutland is Funen, the middle island in Denmark's three main land masses. We go to try our luck in it's biggest city, Odense.

A one man band is playing on one of the streets when we're walking around looking for a pitch, he seems to be doing pretty well. The other walkways seem good too, there's a lot of people in town. We find a space, set up and play. The local shops love it, a cafe brings us a coffee almost immediately, the guy from the chocolate shop next door walks over to give us a sweet treat to go with it. If only that was a positive sign but we're running on good will alone because after an hour and a half the guitar case is still relatively empty, no more than about five pounds in change. We call it a day and make our way back to the van.

The one man band is still playing, filling the street with the big sound of a full band all on his own. He's still doing okay, he's working hard for it too. Feet and elbows moving like an engine to play a full drum kit strapped to his back, strumming an acoustic guitar, singing and blowing into a harmonica on a rack in front of his mouth.

When he pauses between songs we go and say hi. He's from Wales, the accent unmistakeable. Steve Hart, well over six foot tall, a restless energy, pork pie hat tilted back on top of his large smiling face, red flowery shirt. He married a Danish lady after years of busking around Europe, they settled here and have three sons. He's a full-time busker and does comedy magic shows too. The whole family are taking a trip soon so he can play a street music festival in Austria,

"Oh, which one?"

"You won't have heard of it, a tiny town called Feldkirch."

How about that, it's the one we're booked for.

No need for goodbyes,

"See you in Austria in a few weeks."

Steve starts playing again, like a locomotive leaving a railway station, first strumming the guitar, then his legs start going, then the elbows, then the harmonica until he's an unstoppable music machine in motion.

We go back over to Jutland and make our way up north, calling into places on the way, Randers, Viborg, Aalborg, Saeby.

In Frederikshavn, a harbour town that runs ferry services to Sweden and Norway, we collect other Scandinavian coins as well as kroners and euros. The wind whips from the seafront into the main square, we have to find places that give us shelter from it. In the refuge of an empty shopfront, a tall well dressed gentleman comes up and wants to buy one of our CD's. He's shy and asks, as people sometimes do, if it's actually us on the recording. When we say yes, he takes one, says thank you and leaves.

Then he writes to us soon afterwards, asks if we remember him and says he enjoyed meeting us, is enjoying our CD and he would do what he could to let people in Denmark know about us and our music. His name's Tommy, we met another Tommy recently too. He told us it was a popular name in Denmark after the war, parents calling their sons Tommy out of affection for the British soldiers.

There's a festival people keep mentioning, up on the very tip of Jutland, at the end of the peninsula that sticks out at the top of the east coast. Skagen Festival, mostly folk and acoustic music over a long weekend, it's just starting.

As we drive into the centre there are large marquees in and around the town and the harbour. Hoards of people making their way between the two. We pull into a supermarket to get some shopping. There's never usually a time limit in the car parks but this one in town says you can only stay for an hour. I make a note of the time and we go in, we've got a list but Jayne always says,

"Don't look at the list until the end."

She doesn't like to walk around the shop with our eyes glued to a bit of paper. Along one of the aisles I see digestive biscuits, how about that, a taste of home. On the packet, something I've never seen before, advice to the buyer, 'this product does not aid the process of digestion'.

We make sure we're out in good time but on the windscreen is a ticket, the official kind, a parking fine. That can't be right, we've only been half an hour, if that. We're from England, we know about restrictions and time limits when we leave our van parked anywhere. The traffic warden is in the corner of the parking lot, getting in his car to leave, the logo on the side of his vehicle the same as the one on the ticket. We get to him just before he turns the ignition, tell him we've definitely not been here for an hour. He's sorry, explains we need a parking disc in our window to show our time of arrival, without one they don't know how long we've been here and we get a ticket. Our details have been put in his machine, it's been logged now, there's nothing he can do. He apologises, tells us to write to head office and gives us a parking disc of our own to avoid the problem next time.

On the ticket there's an email address in small print at the bottom, a private firm based in Copenhagen. We send a polite note asking for forgiveness, say we're on holiday in their beautiful country and are sorry for our British ignorance of the rules in their car park. Also that we definitely didn't overstay the time limit.

Skagen is a small town but it's in full swing with the festival, the summer season and the tourists. The cafes and restaurants all have outdoor seating, big umbrellas, extra stations for selling beer, queues out of the door of every ice cream parlour. The centre of town is a pedestrian crossroads. An eight piece eastern European band are playing on the corner. Gypsy style music with clarinets, violins and a keyboard. I can tell they're going to be there for the duration, some of them are sat on chairs, they have a table with albums on. When a member of the public shows an interest in the CD's the band leader stops playing and goes over, doffing his hat, bowing slightly.

Down the street from the crossroads to the harbour there's a busker with a silvery white beard, a leather flat cap, the physique of a father Christmas. Sat on a wooden box with an acoustic guitar, microphone and small amp, his case is full of a good amount of change. I think we might've seen him far off up a street in another town a couple of days ago. We keep walking past him as we're trying to find a pitch, whenever we do, he isn't playing, he's chatting to passers by. We figure we won't be interrupting if we do the same. He's got a strong Liverpudlian accent, tells us he has a van he lives in, travels up to Denmark and Skagen every year from Germany. He's reluctant to reveal where he goes, which towns he plays in. Probably thinks that if he tells us then we'll go there ourselves, and to be fair, we probably would. As we're talking someone calls out,

"The Norwegians are coming."

There's a sound of horns honking further up the street. Coming down the road towards us is a convoy of old tractors, people are moving to the side, cheering and clapping. Each of the tractors is pulling trailers carrying men in old fashioned suits and traditional work clothes, cans of beer in one hand, waving to the crowds with the other. Little Norwegian flags are flapping on the end of poles attached to each vehicle. Our conversation has to stop, people are shouting, tractor engines are spluttering their deep throaty tiger's purr. As the last one passes, the noise subsides, our friend says the festival hasn't officially started until the Norwegians arrive. We say goodbye and he softens and leans towards us,

"The town of Lokken on the west coast is good on market day."

Our best busking session is in the evening

on the pedestrian route leading out of the centre. People staggering home, happy, lazy, linking arms, some of them still carrying cans of beer. They're in a good mood and have plenty of change left in their pockets.

Back at the van there's an email from the parking firm in Copenhagen, to help them with their enquiry they need our address. Okay. Wait a minute, they don't know our address. What are they going to do, they can't write to us or send us anything? We write back and say it's no use giving them an address, we won't be there for months. They don't reply and we never hear from them again.

One of the campsites in Skagen has coin operated showers. We discover it by accident when we're looking around, wondering whether to pay the peak season price to cram into a packed holiday park just to use the facilities. Back at the van we put a stack of 5 kroner coins in our pockets, towels and clean clothes in a day rucksack. Undercover and on a mission, a mission to infiltrate a family camping resort, get clean, leave without attracting attention. We rendezvous back outside the gates, wet hair, guilty look on our faces, trying to look like day trippers off to the beach, a little buzz of adrenaline running through our veins.

There are little collections of summer houses and campsites all down the west coast, the Danish flag flying on top of long white poles anywhere where there's a resort or more than a few houses grouped together. Long stretches of wide sandy beaches along the North Sea, some of them you can drive your car on. The Germans and the Danes can spend a day on the beach, either sat in or next to the car to shelter from the wind.

In the little town of Lønstrup we drive past a small music theatre attached to a cafe. The theatre's painted sky blue with flashes of yellow, it's name's written in a Parisian style font over the front door. Customers are sat outside on the terrace in the sunshine. We go in for coffee. When the owner brings it over we tell him we're musicians and happy to play a gig if there's any chance he'd like to book us.

"Drink your coffee, we'll talk in a minute."

When he's finished serving other customers he comes over and sits with us. He has a Salvador Dali moustache, neatly waxed and curled into circles at both ends, his name's Anker. When he talks the moustache is mesmerising, it sits on top of a grin that exposes his teeth on one side. Grinning is something he does regularly, Anker likes to joke, heavy irony, you have to pause and check if he's being serious. Yes, he's up for us playing a gig, he'll pay us by putting 5 kroner, around 50p, on the price of everything he sells during the concert and give us that as our cut.

Anker feeds us and gives us drinks too, a little crowd come along in the evening for the music and to eat in the cafe. At the end of the night, after we've finished the last song, he gives a speech in Danish to everyone that's come along. There's a round of applause, then he turns to us with a cheeky grin and says,

"What are you doing tomorrow night?"

His mischievous Cheshire cat smile and moustache, but he's being serious. The car park in town is comfortable enough so we hang out another day and play the next night too.

One more stop on our way out of Denmark, the gig at the restaurant by the picnic tables. The nearest town to it is Odder but it's not pronounced anything like it looks. We know because whenever we've told someone about it, had polite conversations with people curious to know where we're going, no one's heard of the place. But this isn't true, it's because we're saying it wrong. Turns out you pronounce Odder more like you're expressing distaste for something that makes your stomach turn over. The word starts in your throat then projects forward on your tongue as you curl it up and stick it out slightly while opening your mouth. That's what it seems but try as we might we can't replicate the sound and have to go through the same misunderstandings each time until they realise the place we're talking about.

Pulling into the little car park it's as idyllic as we remember. The wild grass, the low cliff edge, a short path down to a beach, little sailing boats resting on the shoreline.

The restaurant itself is small, a little L shaped

one storey building, enough room for the open plan kitchen and twenty covers but it's the summer and everyone's eating outside. Muted green metal tables and chairs spread spaciously over dark coloured decking looking out through some trees to the grass and the panoramic sea beyond.

The owner and chef is in the kitchen, pans on open flames behind him, saucepans of boiling water bubbling away, two neat looking plates of food are ready to go out, he rings the bell. His name's Bjørn, if there's anything we need just ask one of the waitresses he says as we step aside to let one of them take the two meals ready to go out. He starts plating up again, no coincidence that Bjørn means bear in Danish, with his short solid frame he's got the look of a Viking with his big beard, shaved head, black apron, beads of sweat on his brow from the hot kitchen.

We're playing outside, enjoying the same view as the diners, the blue summer evening sky, the swallows flying over the wild grass. As it gets darker, the blues in the sky and sea get deeper and the temperature drops a little. Blankets get brought out for customers to keep warm. A lady comes over and says she's on holiday at a nudist colony down the road, do we live around here as we should get in touch with them about a gig.

"Would we have to play naked?"

"Of course."

We tell her it's our last day in Denmark today, time and circumstance have removed the dilemma.

I've never even thought about whether I'd play a gig naked, I'm at an advantage with an acoustic guitar compared to Jayne's ukulele. Or maybe not, when I first met her she was modelling nude for life drawing classes. Maybe it would depend on what they were paying? It sets us on a discussion for the rest of the evening but we can't reach a conclusion about what we'd do.

The little car park is quiet by the time we've packed up and climbed into the back of the van, just a couple of cars left that belong to the staff. They're in a happy mood, the sound of them laughing and joking carries in the air as they finish cleaning and preparing for tomorrow. The sky is black and starry now, there's no moon tonight or else it's well hidden by dark clouds we can't see.

Lying in bed I can hear the last of their voices, car doors slamming, a shaft of light spills onto the ceiling from the headlights, the sound of wheels on the gravel as they pull away. Bjørn said if we come back to Denmark to let him know, we can arrange more gigs. Maybe we will, maybe we could come again next summer. We haven't done so bad for a spontaneous trip, we scored a gig at a cafe and a restaurant, played a wedding and had some luck on the streets. More money in our purse now than when we got here.

Quite how we did it we don't know but we

got booked for Linz again, the same as last year. The whole length of Germany to travel through to get there, around 700 miles between Denmark and Austria, by the second day we've carved up a good part of the journey.

Every time we stop at a service area there's no chance of missing the big news of the day. Newspapers and TV screens everywhere showing the painted faces of football fans flying the German flag, in kits, national scarves, hats, images of the iconic gold trophy. It's the football world cup final, it's tonight and Germany are playing against Argentina.

There has to be some big screen showing the game. We come off the motorway and drive through a couple of small towns but they're not big enough to have anything going on. Back on the motorway, what's the next city? Regensburg, got to be something happening there. Regensburg's on the Danube, the city centre on its south side, in the middle of the river there's an elongated island with green parkland and a free car park. Whatever happens we can sleep the night here, other camper vans are doing the same, lots of cars too. We walk in over the bridge and as we're crossing we can see to the left below us, a huge outdoor television screen. Some sort of mock up of a sandy beach complete with deck chairs, umbrellas, a bar and restaurant. There's tiered seating arranged for viewing the match. Five euros to get in, a drink included in the entry price.

We take our drinks to the seats, the match starts, everyone's in a good mood, excitable German voices all around us but at the end of the first half nobody's scored.

Rain starts to fall on our sandy beach in the interval, enough to put people off returning to the tiered seats which are now wet and empty. We stand up for the second half, still no goals, the excitement and energy turning into tension and anticipation, the people around us mostly quiet now. As the referee blows the final whistle the crowd lets out a collective groan, still no goals. Extra time, this is turning into a marathon, the drizzling rain has made the air cold, harder to be comfortable, standing for so long, shifting my weight from one leg to the other. There might be a penalty shoot out at the end to decide the winners. Then in the second half of extra time Germany scores! The crowd goes wild, ecstatic, all the pent up tension released in a moment. The last few minutes still have to play out, anything could happen but there are no more goals. Germany 1 – Argentina 0. Everybody goes crazy.

We're more excited to stretch our legs, we're glad they've won but hadn't planned on needing that much stamina. The rain has stopped and the nation is coming out to celebrate. Cars stream into the city, blocking every road, people waving flags, honking horns, hanging out of windows. In the city centre we get caught in a huge crowd that keeps erupting into mass chanting. We're just spectators though, the celebrations are all theirs, after an hour we squeeze our way out and make our way back over the bridge. Lucky that the Danube stands between us and the party on the other side.

One of the performers at Pflasterspektakel says she goes to the Edinburgh Festival every year to busk on the streets. She has a circle act, one of the shows that draws a crowd, climaxes with her on top of a short ladder juggling three knives. Edinburgh Fringe have an application for street artists, it's online, she says it's easy to get in, you get your performance times once you're there.

We look at the diary over the next month, we could go to Edinburgh in about three weeks time, after a couple of gigs in Lincoln. She's right, the application is easy, we choose three days and they send confirmation straight back that we're in.

One more festival in Europe still to go, the other side of Austria next weekend. We drive half the way there and stop at a campsite by a lake but it's the summer holidays and the place is overflowing. They have a space for us, we book in, it's cramped, we've neighbours close by on both sides. Their big tents are pitched right beside their cars, roof racks, bicycles, canoes and inflatables, it's hard not to listen to their every movement, close enough to smell the sunscreen and every sizzling thing that goes on their barbecue.

We ditch the idea of staying and decide

just to go to Feldkirch where the festival is, we'll find somewhere there. The town is tucked into the western edge of Austria, by the borders of Liechtenstein and Switzerland. There's got to be somewhere we can stay but when we get to the town every campsite is full! No space anywhere. It looks like there's another camping place a couple of kilometres away, out by the Rhine River, right by the bridge over to Switzerland. When we get there, a track leads off the road and down into the campsite but you can see straight away it isn't a public one, it's some sort of boy scout camp. We pull up on the grass verge, we've run out of ideas. There's a house on the roadside, a mother and daughter sat outside on the porch, they're looking over, smiling. We go and say hi, the daughter speaks good English, she's in her late teens, do they know any campsites? We tell them the ones in town are full, we're here to play at the festival at the weekend.

"Wait a minute, I will ring my father."

The daughter disappears inside the house for a few minutes then comes back out,

"I talked with my father, you can stay here, it's no problem."

She points to the area of grass where we're parked, their side garden, looking out over the Rhine. We're strangers and they've offered to let us camp outside their house on their land. They bring out a tray of tea and we sit around and talk. They're from Romania, the father's a lawyer, the daughter loves to sing, she's the eldest of three, they're on their summer holidays from school.

We make our own little camping area, chairs and table by the side door to the van. Now and again we see the family coming or going, exchange a friendly wave. It's good for walking too, three different countries in one stroll. We can cross the bridge into Switzerland, go down the river to the next bridge, cross over into Liechtenstein and then up the track home to Austria.

The festival organisers have a hotel in town for us and we can check in on Thursday. With no distance to travel we're pretty much the first to arrive. The reception staff don't waste time with niceties, they probably save them for the people that are paying the bill. Another act arrives just after us, they get the same treatment, still, we get what we need, our room key and the timings for breakfast.

Feldkirch is a pretty town centred around a long cobbled market square that's overlooked by historic four storey buildings, each one a different colour. Porticos run the length of both sides, an old church at one end, a fountain, lots of cafes with outdoor seating, small alleys leading in and out. Perfect for a street performer's festival.

Most of the pitches are good but some are a little out of the way, the further out from the middle the less people you attract. Our last slot on Friday is one of these, a laid-back corner opposite a small restaurant a couple of streets from the main square, not much footfall. There's some tables outside the restaurant but they're behind large pots of foliage.

The diners can't see us, we can't see them, just the head and shoulders of a well dressed waiter as he comes in and out.

When we finish playing a gentleman stands up from one of the tables behind the flower pots and comes over,

"Do you have time to join my wife and I for a drink?"

The waiter brings extra chairs to their little table, takes orders for drinks for us and our hosts, Rupi and Kati. Rupi, he says, is short for Ruprecht, but he likes to be called Prince Rupi, enjoys the joke and the idea of a royal title. He has the hair of an ageing prince too, slightly wavy, shoulder length, swept back and down both sides. His brown rimmed glasses give him the look of a professor but bookishness is superseded by his bonhomie. His English is perfect, Kati's is good too but she doesn't think it is.

They're here from Berlin, on a kind of working holiday. Prince Rupi's an opera critic, there's an opera house up the road in Bregenz, they're surprised we've not heard of it. Famous for being on the lake, the stage floats on the water, the auditorium's on the land. They went last night to see Mozart's *The Magic Flute*, it's on for the next few weeks. In fact, Prince Rupi says, it would be a perfect place for busking before the show, opera tickets are so expensive that most people who buy one want to make an evening of it. The show doesn't start until the sun goes down, around 9pm, when the stage lighting can become effective. There's a long stretch of early evening before that, everyone parading along the promenade in their finest, going to waterfront restaurants, eating, drinking and passing the time. He thinks we'd do well. He also says we can come and stay with them if we're ever in Berlin.

The next day it rains. It really rains. We cover all our kit in bin liners and wheel it into town. The organisers say there'll be no timetable today, it's a free for all, you can go anywhere you like, play anywhere it's possible to play. Also the finale to the festival, the big showcase, is cancelled as it's outside but we'll all meet up later to have something to eat together.

We play under a shop canopy for a while, the water dripping off the front like a rain curtain. A few people come out into the town in wet weather gear, they stop for a while under the canopies on the opposite side, watching us with their wet faces. We exchange shrugs across the road, our eyes turning up to the sky. If they have children they send them to put money in the case. Their wellington boots head straight for the puddles in the middle of the street, splashing through to cross over, splashing again to get back. We last for an hour, that's enough. Even wheeling everything back to the hotel things get wet, we put the heating on in our room despite it being the middle of summer and dry it all off.

In the evening we go to the after party to eat and say our farewells. Steve Hart, the one man band we met in Odense is here, he's brought his family, his wife and three sons came down in their car from Denmark. His boys are teenagers, long legs, the genes of future basketball players. Steve's a seasoned busker, never put off by the weather, he's played all day today, even doing a turn in the local butchers, he did pretty well, his boys collecting the money for him. Steve says if we want to come up to Denmark again he could probably organise five or six concerts for us.

Sunday morning, the rain has gone like it was never even here, just blue skies and warm sunshine again. We drop our room key at reception and check out, the staff more enthusiastic with the goodbyes than they were with the hellos. Prince Rupi's advice about the opera, we've been talking about it all through breakfast. Austrian cities are normally a no go for busking but if we're on the promenade, who knows, maybe we'll get away with it, it's only twenty miles from here and on our route back anyway.

Bregenz sits on the side of Lake Constance. There's a long promenade meandering for over a mile through parks, green spaces and harbour areas. A ferry terminal, restaurants, pavilions and the opera house, The Seebühne, the floating stage. Bregenz feels affluent, wealthy and well kept. We follow the directions to the big lakeside car parks but the place is full, no spaces. Back over the bridge that crosses the train line, separating the waterfront from the city, there's a supermarket. Doesn't seem to be any restrictions, we'll walk in from here.

We head straight for the opera house. It's impressive, you can see through open doors into the auditorium and out onto the water. Three giant horned dragon-like creatures, maybe a hundred foot tall, connected by roped bridges and towering over a domed stage. Showtime is hours away but the concourse, the huge open space in front of the opera house is busy. Big white industrial sized marquees serving champagne and round pretzels the size of steering wheels, smart waiters and waitresses, staff with walkie talkies. Crowds wandering through, and just like us, stopping to take a look at the spectacle.

On the periphery of the opera, just past the marquees, restaurants and ice cream stalls there's a small harbour. Rows of little boats tied up on the jetties, blue, red and yellow pedaloes for tourists to take short trips out on the lake. Seems like as good a place as any, we're not in anyone's way, the waterfront here is just for strolling.

Rupi's right, people are doing exactly that, they're out walking but they're taking their time. You can tell by how well dressed they are whether they're going to the opera or not. We set up in front of the railings, with our backs to the pedal boats and play. Little crowds stop to watch, no one's in a hurry, they have time to look and listen to this curious impromptu entertainment. We play short shows, twenty minutes or so to allow people to gather and then move on. Each time we finish they politely come and give money and buy CD's, happy to be momentarily diverted before they stroll on.

The amount of refined evening wear increases, our audiences have never been so well dressed. Expensive tailored suits, cufflinks and tie pins, silk handkerchiefs in top pockets, linen outfits, jewellery, the smell of high end perfume. Generous too, it's hard not to keep looking at the guitar case and the amount of euros we're collecting in there. How many CD's have we sold so far? I've lost count.

By eight o'clock the strollers are picking up their pace, moving quicker as it gets closer to showtime, the late arrivals eager to get to their seats. They no longer have the time, no one wants to hang around any more, we take it as our cue to pack up.

Back at the supermarket car park, it's empty, just our van and a couple of cars left. An attendant with a big bunch of keys waves at us then taps his watch, they're locking the gates, we just made it. We drive closer to the centre of town, plenty of change in our pockets to pay for a space. Under the overhead light in the front seat we count up our earnings. Just over 300 euros. How about that? We've never made anything like this before. A celebration is called for, we take a table at an Italian restaurant in town and drink a toast to Prince Rupi and Kati.

Afterwards we can't resist walking back to the waterfront. The night sky is dark azure, the lake has turned black. There's still people about, wandering in and out of the shadows, in and out of the pools of light coming from the circular street lamps all along the promenade. We stop for a minute at the spot where we played, lean on the railings and look out over the lake, a little breeze cooling the warm night air. I can hear the sound of the opera in the distance, getting louder, swells of symphonic drama.

Further along you can glimpse an oblique view of the rear of the floating stage on the water. There's a gathering of people, some have brought fold-up chairs to watch this small slice of the performance, a peak at the towering dragons bathed in red and green lights. The music comes to a climax, a crescendo, then the long, long applause of a well pleased audience before they pour out onto the walkways. Thousands of opera leavers, some in a hurry, first out of the gate, briskly heading to the car parks and coaches to avoid the jams. Others take their time, the staff in the marquees are poised and ready with more champagne and pretzels.

We still have a day in hand for our drive to catch the ferry, maybe we'll come back again tomorrow.

11. MOODY FRIED EGG

The next morning, Monday, and it's raining, the forecast says it'll carry on all day. Reluctantly we make the decision to leave Bregenz, leave that golden ticket behind and start the journey home. Later on we find out the opera doesn't even show on a Monday anyway!

We cross over to Dover from Dunkirk, someone tipped us off that the route is less popular and cheaper than going from Calais. It takes half an hour longer but this is a bonus for us, one and a half hours is barely time to get on board, settle down and tuck into our new favourite ferry meal. Chips and beans. We're a couple of big kids again with our school dinners, sachets of salt, vinegar and ketchup. Like unaccompanied children we kick our legs under the bucket seats of our plastic table by the window, looking back at the big white wake of the ship as it ploughs through the English Channel.

Up to Lincoln, back to the funky bar in the basement of the hotel. This was a triumph last year, the place full to the rafters. Jayne's invited three friends from Grimsby, they're excited to come and see us and have listened into another interview we did this afternoon on local radio. We'd be excited to see them too if it weren't for the fact that they're the only three faces in the audience.

They've sat right in front of us, in the centre of emptiness. Over my shoulder I can see our poster from the gig last year on the wall, a testimonial to an evening that couldn't have been more different. Our signatures written in black marker pen along with tributes about how great that night was, what a fabulous evening people had.

At The Strugglers on Sunday, a chip butty in my hand at half-time, someone says the buzz around that venue faded, the gigs no longer attract much interest. Then they ask,

"Where are you going next?"

"We're playing at the Edinburgh Fringe."

I can hear the words coming out of my mouth, it sounds a little inflated, pretentious even. Exciting, adventurous, but a bit overblown, the reality is anybody's guess.

For a start it's five hours away. After Newcastle, the last one hundred miles is all single carriageway and we do something we don't usually do and sleep the night in a lay-by. For the main road to Scotland on the west it's surprisingly quiet, quiet enough for me to stand in the middle of the road in the morning and take a photo of us parked up. Looking back down at us tucked into the single lane of a lay-by, the open road, white clouds overhead, blue sky in the background, mist and darker skies behind me.

Edinburgh however is another matter. After driving round for ages looking for a parking spot we squeeze into one in the suburbs to the north of Holyrood Park. No restrictions here, if we're subtle about it I think we can stay for the three days. There's a high garden wall to our immediate left and a block of flats on the other side of the road. No reason we would attract any curtain twitchers, it's the Edinburgh Festival after all, the busiest time of the year. We're half a mile from the Scottish Parliament, then it's another half a mile up the hill to the Royal Mile and the city centre.

The next morning I inch back the curtain to see what kind of day it is before sitting at the bottom of the bed to make coffee. Jayne saw me taking a peak outside,

"What's the weather like?"

"Moody fried egg."

Years ago she was on holiday with a friend. The friend's daughter wore a dress with white and yellow circles on it. The young girl was usually sunny and happy but one day was down in the dumps. She was wearing the little fried egg patterned dress and in a spontaneous attempt to cheer her up, 'Moody Fried Egg' was born. It got the little girl smiling again and from then on it's been a way of describing anything, from someone's behaviour to a gloomy state of affairs, particularly the weather, overcast skies being the perfect example.

We walk up the long hill into the city, heavy grey clouds are threatening to release a bucket load of rain. Signs of the Edinburgh Festival everywhere, not just in the banners and posters but the amount of young people in the centre handing out flyers, advertising and promoting shows in any way they can. Busy beyond belief, regular city goers along with festival goers, on top of all that the tourists and day trippers. Lots of them aren't here for the festival though, you can tell by the way they're walking around the Royal Mile like they're on safari, curious but wary. Add to this the street artists, big circle shows, fire, daredevil and circus acts and you have total chaos.

Why we thought it would be a good idea to come and busk as part of the Fringe I've no idea. Maybe the sunshine and summer heat went to our heads, maybe the generous public at the festival in Austria got us thinking it might be the same here.

There's a festival general office, a headquarters, all the registered buskers have to turn up in the morning to get their slot, split into two groups, the circle shows on one side and everyone else including us, on the other. Ours is a varied bunch, guys and girls with guitars, jugglers, puppeteers, there's no filter or curation, just first come first serve. The slots are thirty minutes long which includes setting up and packing down, all of them are in and around the central section of the high street, the heavily congested hub of the festival and Edinburgh itself. We're given a lanyard that shows we're official, on it are the words, 'This pass doesn't give me super powers!' Maybe egos have got too big in the past, the temptation to tie on a cape and jump off a roof has been too strong.

Our time slot comes around, along with the time slots of loads of other performers as well, two of whom are twenty metres away on either side of us. We turn up the volume to try and be heard amidst the noise and chaos but the marshals are vigilant. They carry signs to show if you're too loud and they flash one at us to turn it down, a circular sign showing a red face with a downturned mouth.

It's a relief to get to the end. How a couple of people heard us and came out of the crowd to put a coin in the case I don't know. We take the two coins out of the case and pack everything away, go back down the hill to our little home on wheels parked up in the suburbs.

We've seen online that there are showers at Edinburgh railway station, £5 each. In the evening we try to share one but the attendant won't allow it, we have to have one each. Worth it just to wash off the city centre dirt at the end of the day. We've signed up to play for three days but there's no way we're going in to relive that experience again, with or without super powers. As we walk back, damp hair and damp towels, I tell myself maybe sleep'll put more distance between us and the feeling of being in the wrong place at the wrong time.

Next day we decide to get back on the

horse, go in, avoid the central hub, avoid the official organised spots, find somewhere else, maybe salvage something from the situation. There's a quieter part of the city, Edinburgh New Town, shops and restaurants, away from the main tourist attractions, away from most of the big festival events too. Even wheeling the trolley around it's better, we're not surrounded by mayhem and there's no competition, just casual shoppers and diners. We can play when we like, for as long as we like and we can hear ourselves.

Rays of sunshine sometimes pierce through the clouds, single shafts of light that hint at turning the weather around but the wind soon blows the gaps closed. More coins thrown in the case today but not enough to make it worthwhile staying and we decide to cut our losses and leave town. As we drive away the sky darkens, deep shades of grey turning black, threatening to rain again. Moody fried egg.

We zigzag our way south again, revisiting places that will have us, ones that are easy to rebook. In Loughborough we're booked to play a charity gig so we check into a campsite the day before, it rains all day, and the next day too so we just sit it out, grateful to have a gig in the evening.

The campsite's informal, not many people, the rain coming down across empty pitches. We decide to stay on site during the day rather than sit and wait in some supermarket car park. Checkout time is late morning and we overshoot it, at 2pm I go to the office. Standing in my rain soaked jacket, shaking the drips off, I tell the young receptionist our situation,

"Is it okay to hang out here before we head off?"

"Seems like you've already made you're mind up."

The charity gig is upstairs in the function room of a pub out of town, £5 ticket price and the money goes to Oxfam. Looking at who's on the bill Jayne recognises a name from her past, from years ago, back when she went to a folk club in Grimsby. Vicky Clayton, she used to perform there, maybe she'll remember you I suggest,

"That was 30 years ago, I was only in the audience."

As we're talking at the sound desk Vicky walks in, long blonde hair, wearing floaty clothes from the sixties, big costume jewellery. She spots us and comes over, says to Jayne,

"I'm sure I recognise you from somewhere."

Vicky calls everyone "Darlin'" and plays the role of mother hen for the night, encouraging everyone, whether they're coming on or off stage. The audience are quiet, attentive, listening, they've paid to get in.

Our sketch of a plan is to drive down through France again, busking in towns and cities on the way until we get to Italy. Someone tipped us off there's a truffle festival in Alba where it's good for playing on the street. This year we'll make better use of the weather, we'll be earlier than last year, before it turns too cold. All we've got to do is earn enough to make it through to when it's time to go to Dervla's in Ireland. Try to fill the envelope with enough euros to hole up for the coldest of the winter months.

Chips and beans on the early morning ferry to France. A chance to look closer at the route we might take, towns we might chose to try our luck at. String them all together like a constellation, join the dots between Dunkirk in France and Alba in Italy.

First we go to Amiens, big enough for us to change to a new spot every hour all afternoon. There's a good amount of euro coins getting thrown in the case, the sound of each one clinking against the others as it drops in, convincing us we might do okay in France. An immaculately dressed air hostess, bright red lipstick and pinned up hair stops to talk and buys two of our CD's. We're getting good vibes from being here and we're one long baguette and a couple of cold drinks heavier when we take our gear back to the van.

Finding somewhere to stay is pretty easy, lots of towns and villages, even small ones, have an Aire du Camping Car, a car park for visitors to stay overnight. There's one halfway between Amiens and Saint-Quentin, two big towns only an hour from each other. This is easy travelling, we can save our energy for playing.

In Saint-Quentin there's a grand square in the town centre, a huge oversized space bordered by some important looking colonnaded buildings. One of the corners opens into a kind of mini piazza with a fountain, a couple of bars and a restaurant with outdoor seating. We set up near the fountain in earshot of the diners sat at the outside tables. With people eating and drinking we know we'll have to put the time in, the ones that want to give will wait until they leave, wallets and purses opened up from paying the bill, maybe they'll keep a little something aside for us. As time goes by some of them come out of the restaurant and make their way over,

"Merci pour la musique."

"Merci beaucoup," we say, with a little bow. Some stop and say something in French. If we don't understand, we tell them we're English, Jayne gives Italian as another choice of language but if we've none in common they give us a smile and say,

"Bonne chance."

Good luck. We like Saint-Quentin, it's a big town shrunk down and compacted around a gigantic central square, the people seem polite and appreciative. A lady comes over from a table outside the bar opposite. She's been drinking, her face is red, her eyes wet, her lipstick a little smudged but she's friendly and invites us back to her apartment to cook us a meal. We think about it but hold back from going too fast in our relationship with Saint-Quentin. In that moment we decide to come back again tomorrow, we tell her if she's in town at the same time again we'll catch her then. She seems happy enough with this, her head moving up and down and side to side in a way that says it's the second best option. Back at her table on the other side of the street, the barman brings her another drink. One of those orange coloured aperitifs the French love in the early evening, she lights a cigarette and lifts her glass up to us.

That's it then, we'll come back again tomorrow. There's a municipal campsite not far from the bottom of the hill that leads down out of town, a little north along the canal. The reviews aren't great but it's cheap and there's hot showers.

It's a youth hostel run by the local council, a flat camping ground around it, a few trees, one brick toilet block outside for the campers, all utilitarian, designed to handle large volumes of people. Lucky there are hardly any at the moment, we're out of the summer season now, into early autumn. Easy enough to pitch up, get clean, cook a meal. Counting up the money we can put some in the winter envelope already, we might be finding our rhythm with this.

The next day I tell the manager in the hostel that we'll stay another night. Neither of us speak the same language, he keeps a straight face but I think he gets the idea when I roll my hands around themselves to indicate an ongoing situation. Leaving our table and chairs at the pitch we drive along the canal to put us nearer to the town, there's free parking opposite the police station.

We unload our gear, start walking in with it, a spring in our step, a little buzz of anticipation as I look up at the blue sky, the sunshine and a fresh new day ahead. The feeling of knowing where we're going, what we're doing, why we're doing it. At the bottom of the hill, before we make our way up to town, we have to navigate a roundabout. The easiest way is to the left where there's an extra wide section of pavement, one part of it slightly higher than the other. We're talking, the energy high in our voices as I bump the trolley at an angle over the small kerb, the wheels easily jump up and I swerve between some low standing bollards.

Jayne's walking on my right but doesn't see the little step and her foot gets caught on the side of it sending her off balance. She trips and falls, reaching out quickly but her hand doesn't make it in time. The weight of her body falls on her wrist against one of the little black bollards and she cries out in pain. Getting up you can see that it's bad, really bad. Her left wrist is in an unfamiliar shape, crooked and bent, much longer than normal. She's crying and holding it with her right hand, tears running down her face, we're staring at it in shock and disbelief. This is serious, this needs a hospital right away. How do you call an ambulance in France? I don't know.

Two young guys are walking past, they can see there's a problem, they can hear there's a problem. They come over, you don't need words to describe the situation, Jayne walking round and round in circles, sobbing and cursing, her right hand clutching her bent left wrist. They call an ambulance. I wish I could do something to help but nothing's going to soothe the pain. In what seems like no time at all I hear the siren of an ambulance, it appears at the roundabout, weaves through the cars that have pulled over and parks on the pavement next to us. The paramedics jump out, there's no doubt who the patient is and they put Jayne straight in the back. I have the trolley so I can't go with them, they tell me where they're going and speed off.

Bloody hell! What just happened. One minute we're strolling into a friendly French town, the next, Jayne's in the back of an ambulance. No doubt she's broken her wrist, really properly broken it too, you don't need to be a medic to see that. She's in agony, what she must be going through I don't know, what thoughts she might be thinking. So much to take in, is she going to be okay, will she be able to play again? The road's risen up to meet us, suddenly and violently.

I drive to the Saint-Quentin hospital, park up in a street adjacent and make my way to the A&E department. By the time I get there they've put Jayne in a small room on her own, she's sitting up in bed, a white gown on, a blue paper sling cradling her left arm. There's a drip feeding into her right wrist. She looks vulnerable, fragile, everyone does in this situation, she manages a smile, the pain killers have kicked in. All she knows is that she's waiting to go into surgery, they've got her ready. That's about it, the language barrier has meant she hasn't understood much of it. We sit and wait, the room's a sanitised oasis, calm. Outside the corridors are busy, doctors and nurses passing left and right, moving with purpose. An hour later and two of them come and wheel her out.

After the operation they put Jayne in a ward on the seventh floor, in a bed by the window. She's sleepy and tired but says she's been told they've put two pins in to hold her wrist in place, big ones that you can feel just under the skin. They'll need to come out in a couple of months. No plaster on her wrist though, no cast or anything, just a crepe bandage held on with a safety pin. So delicate, her tender forearm held in a thin cloth and a blue paper sling. I sit in the chair next to her and hold her other hand, we're just looking at each other, taking turns now and again to slowly shake our heads.

The nurses on the ward distract us, cheerful as their feet bounce and squeak around on the floor in their thick rubber soled shoes. One of them loves The Beatles. We exchange song lyrics each time we see her, lines from the best known verses as she recalls her favourite songs, says she loves all things British. Not something I expected to hear in France but the Beatles lyrics sound good in her heavy French accent. It keeps her coming back regularly to check on Jayne before she bounces and squeaks off again down the corridor.

I lose track of the time, only noticing how many hours must have passed when there's no light coming in any more from outside. Just the big square fluorescent lights on the ceiling, the windows are black now, unless I stand up and look out at the street lamps lighting the suburbs of Saint-

Quentin. The darkness turns the window into a mirror, reflecting the room back to me, a stark and unwanted reminder of where we are.

Later they turn the overhead light off too, only the cold glow of a reading lamp floods the bed, I'm sitting in the shadows, the rest of the room's in darkness. I think I've been forgotten about, maybe I can sleep right here in the chair but on her next round the nurse tells me I have to leave. I say a quiet goodnight to Jayne and make my way out, the corridors are quiet, the elevator drops me silently down seven floors. Outside the main entrance an old man in a dressing gown is leaning on a walking stick having a late night cigarette. We exchange a *"bon soir"* as he blows smoke up and out into the cool air. Back at the van I jump in, slam the side door shut and lie down on the bed. Lie looking at the roof, just the sound of an occasional car driving past, my first ever night in here alone.

The ward's busy with the start of a fresh day, the squeak of nurses' shoes up and down the hallways, pacing through lists of things that need to get done. Jayne's sitting up in bed looking brighter, her clothes are folded in a pile on the chair beside her. They're going to release her after a consultation later this morning and I can help her get dressed.

When we start to put her clothes on it's obvious there's going to be a slower pace to life. That delicate wrist only thinly bandaged, nothing else to protect it. The shiny hospital floor suddenly seems hard and unforgiving, it dawns on me that the outside world is also very hard and unforgiving, concrete everywhere, rigid and dangerous. Inflexible rock solid pavements and kerbs. We should really wrap her up in cotton wool and move to a soft play area until she's better, normal life just seems too hazardous.

We say our *au revoirs* and *mercis* to the nurses and walk slowly together through the corridors to her appointment. The consultant says the operation went well, she needs to come back in a week to see how she's getting on. The pins have to come out in about eight weeks, normally they use small ones that can stay in place but her break was so bad they had to use big ones that will need to be removed.

This much we've understood but nobody's said anything about Jayne being a musician, whether she'll be able to play again, what the timescale might be even if she can? We don't know what to think, the language barrier has prevented any of us having a proper conversation about anything apart from Beatles' songs.

Then we're out of the main entrance and into the midday sun, more smokers in dressing gowns puffing away in contemplation. Urban concrete everywhere, the hard reality of tarmac and pavements. Jayne is cautious, walking carefully, I go to hold her hand but realise it means she doesn't have one free for any kind of protection.

When we get to the van she realises for the first time that she can't drive, she's standing by the driver's door, struggling to come to terms with the idea. Trying to think of any possible way she could be the one getting in that seat until her shoulders sink, she surrenders and gets in on the passenger side. I close the door behind her, go round to the driver's seat, together we click her seat belt in, the only thing we know right now is that we've got to be back at the hospital in a weeks time.

Our table and chairs are still where we left them, alone in the middle of the campsite, as if nothing has happened, as if we're just coming back from a day out. They remind me of what life was like yesterday when we left them, only yesterday, it feels a lifetime away. Two tents are pitched out near the edge but no ones around. Quiet, probably nobody noticed that we didn't come back last night, another ordinary unhurried day at the end of the season. I put the kettle on the stove, we sit in silence, there's not much to do apart from think. So many thoughts circling inside my head, too many to contemplate anything for long. I wouldn't make any sense if I tried to articulate them, and anyway Jayne isn't ready to talk yet, what we might do, where we might go. She's tired, she's been through too much, she needs to rest.

The other campers leave the following morning and we're left on our own in the middle. When I go into the youth hostel to pay I notice for the first time it's empty too, the hallway echoes with the sound of the manager as he walks to the front desk, a big bunch of keys jangling in his hand. He puts them down on the counter, raises his eyebrows, the international facial sign of 'what do you want?' I communicate by raising my forefinger, another night, one more night. He's got to be thinking by now, what's with these British people, so indecisive, one minute they're here, then they're not, they don't even know how long they want to stay. He can't wait to take his bunch of keys back down the hallway to do whatever he was doing a few minutes ago.

Maybe we could just carry on with what we were doing, act like this has never happened. Jayne and I start talking, trying to hold on to a life we had this time yesterday. She can still sing, I can play the guitar, we can take things a little slower.

Depending on our mood this plays out in different ways. In one, we're determined adventurers, carrying on regardless, making it work, busking our way down through France into Italy, saving every penny we can, ready to take to Ireland for our house sit this winter. In the other, more daunting version, we're stubbornly going against the grain, avoiding what's obvious, that now isn't the time to be on the road. Which one is it? It's difficult to let go of the idea of carrying on. Difficult because we don't have any kind of backup plan, no nest egg, bolt hole or plan B.

Once we cycled round the Isle of Wight on a couple of second hand bikes and tried to spend the night on a beach. We lit a fire, we had sleeping bags and the weather was good. The tide started to come in but we thought we had a good spot far enough up the beach, the tide'll never come this high. When the water started lapping the edge of the fire, wetting the wood, we relocated some of the embers a bit further up, managing to save enough to keep it going. Surely we were above the high tide mark now. Still the tide kept coming in, the weather turning stormy, the sea becoming volatile and aggressive until we had no choice but to grab everything, rush our bikes up and out. By then the waves were really rough and rowdy, we nearly didn't make it, we nearly got swept away.

It feels like we're sitting on that beach again now, trying to keep the fire of our dreams alight, the water lapping onto the burning wood. I want to ignore the rising tide, pretend we're far enough away from the water's edge and the dark clouds don't mean anything, they're just blowing over. It's really hard to let go, accept the reality of the situation. One things for sure, we need to earn money, the rest of the autumn and the long winter lie ahead and the house sit in Ireland is only a roof over our head.

Talking of a roof over our head, one day in our old basement flat water started dripping heavily through the ceiling. I ran upstairs, rang the doorbell of the guy that lived there. He answered and with some urgency I told him about the water coming through, he said,

"It shouldn't be."

He was right, it shouldn't be, but it was! Just like now, we shouldn't be here, this shouldn't be happening, but it is. The tide's rising, water's coming in! We need an ark, a financial ark for one thing, and a place to be. Jayne needs to be able to get herself better too. What are we going to do about it all, what are we going to do for money, what are we going to do full stop?

The paper sling they've tied around Jayne's arm isn't wearing well, starting to tear and fray, only adjustable by tying a knot tighter behind her neck. We take a slow walk to a nearby chemist and buy a black, Velcro adjustable version, then take a slow walk back.

One minute we're positive, the next we're all doom and gloom, up and down, up and down. Mostly down. The ups are superficial, based on fantastical notions like me getting a job in France. How would that work, how long would it take me to learn basic French, we don't even have an address. Ridiculous, but somehow it plays out in my mind. So much so that I walk to a nearby employment agency displaying vacancies on cards in the window outside. I don't understand any of them.

I find a holiday park online and write to them, seeing if they have any work, thinking that would give us a place to stay and I can do anything that doesn't need me to speak the language. They don't write back. I'm clutching at straws trying to come at our situation from every possible angle. All roads are really pointing back to England, me getting some kind of job, at least temporarily. How would that work though, rent somewhere for a couple of months? That's not really a good option, no one's usually looking for short term lets, who knows what kind of place we'd end up in if they were. Plus we'd be right on the back foot and have immediate bills to cover before I'd even found a job.

The campsite feels wrong now too, nobody else is here, just us parked up in the grounds of a mostly empty municipal building. Maybe if we moved, went somewhere else for a few days before Jayne's hospital appointment. A change of scenery, change our mood, change our thoughts, it feels like we're getting nowhere here. There's one an hour away, in Soissons, I drive us there, Jayne grits her teeth and holds onto the seat with her one free hand.

This one's busier, more people staying, more company, more distractions. Set beside a large woodland park by a river. We can walk on the soft grass, kick our way through the mounting piles of crackly dry red leaves that have fallen from the now bare branches. Autumn is really here.

There's a market square in town, maybe we could try to busk? We see a restaurant that looks like they do live music. The owner speaks a bit of English, she seems positive about a gig and we leave her a card. I think she was just humouring us, the down on our luck look on our faces that we couldn't disguise, Jayne's arm in a sling, not wanting to say no to us there and then. We don't hear anything.

I remember another trip we made on our old second hand bikes, Jayne and I set off from our front door in Hastings and cycled to Paris. We spent the first night in Dieppe in a little tent on a campsite.

In the morning I woke to find a great rip in the side of it, it was a new tent as well. I remember my first thought was, this is going straight back to the shop for a refund when we get home. Turned out it wasn't faulty though. I stood straight up through the gaping hole, the newly sliced side door, every single one of our possessions strewn around the grass outside like there'd been a hurricane. I stepped out, found my trousers, reached into the pocket for our holiday money, 500 euros, the budget for the trip. It was gone! My jeans had been rolled up beside me where I slept. Someone had cut through the side of the tent while we were sleeping, reached in and taken everything out, gone through it all and found the money. We were both in shock, they'd been that close to us in the middle of the night with a knife, rifling through all our belongings, what if we'd woken up? What if I'd used my trousers as a pillow as I often do when we're camping? They'd wanted cash, that much became obvious as they'd not taken anything else, not driving licences, passports, credit cards or ukuleles.

We went to the reception desk, they didn't want to know anything about it, nothing to do with them, they wouldn't call the police either. So we cycled down to the station ourselves and reported it, got a crime reference number. Dazed and confused, reeling with the shock, we hadn't got a clue about what to do next. We did a lot of walking that day, talking it over until eventually we had a realisation. They'd stolen the most unsentimental, replaceable thing, money. It's not a thing until you spend it. So we reported the crime number to the insurance people, threw the tent in the bin and set off on our old bikes for Paris anyway.

It's money we need now though and it doesn't feel so replaceable. Why am I replaying previous disasters? It's not helping, and back then we had proper jobs that put salaries in our account every month, sick pay, house insurance that covered theft away from home, including cash.

We could go and stay on a campsite in England but I'm not sure if I can use it as an address for finding work. I don't mind doing a nine to five job, but the thought of Jayne having to hang around a campsite in our small van all day, all weathers, is miserable. It's September, it's only going to get colder. We keep talking, going back and forth, back and forth, any light that appears at the end of the tunnel soon fades.

There are some films in the van we haven't got round to watching yet so we try to lose ourselves in the movies. *Midnight Cowboy* is the wrong choice. Joe and Ratso, drifters living in a cold and derelict building, down on their luck, hustling, trying to get by on broken dreams.

Each day we ride the roller coaster of our imaginations but like any fairground ride it just goes round and round, never getting us anywhere. My mind races ahead, it wants it to be tomorrow, then the next day and the next until it's all played out and we've moved on to the next chapter and this one's over.

Eventually I do what any bloke in their forties hopes he'll never have to do. I ring my mum, ask her if we can live with her for a bit, just for two months, I can find a job while Jayne's wrist gets mended. She lives in a flat in Eastbourne, of course we can stay she says, no problem. That's it then, we'll go there until our house sit in Ireland starts, try to get enough money earned in a proper job to cover the winter.

After the hospital consultation we drive up and catch the ferry back to England. It feels like the wrong direction to be travelling in, turning round feels like failure. We weren't meant to be going this way, we weren't meant to be back on the ferry so soon. No one's told us anything about how long Jayne's recovery will take either, if she'll even be able to play the ukulele again. The ukulele, it's the reason we're even here in the first place, why we've even ended up doing what we're doing. We never set out to be musicians, everything just happened by chance.

It all started a decade ago, a friend had an old apartment in a tiny village in France, in the foothills of the Pyrenees. He said we could stay there, go for a short holiday break in the winter, there was a fireplace, and just in case to pack a thick jumper or two. When we got there, arriving from the airport in our hire car, it was freezing, the walls of the apartment were a metre thick. We lit the fire but the smoke went everywhere apart from up the chimney until it filled the room and we could barely see our way around. No amount of jumpers were going to keep us warm either.

We had to salvage something from our week away so we drove down to Barcelona, winding our way in, it was all last minute and we didn't even have a map, just drove in, following our nose until we found ourselves a cheap hotel in the middle. On a side street near the hotel was a music shop, in the window was a little wooden ukulele for 30 euros.

That little ukulele led us to buying another one, then forming a ukulele band with the guys next door until we were playing regular gigs. That lead to a three piece band where I switched back to guitar, loads more gigs, functions, weddings, we'd got a taste for it. After a few years we realised the only realistic way of carrying on, travelling further afield, writing our own music, was to do it as the two of us. We never set out that way, weren't confident at first being all on our own, never would've dreamt of doing it if it hadn't been for the purchase of that ukulele. The question now is whether Jayne'll be able to play it again.

My mum's happy to see us when we get to Eastbourne, says we're very welcome, we can share the grocery shopping, no need for any other contributions. She has a small spare room we can stay in.

I just need a job. I've got too much pent up energy to sit at a computer so I go around town on foot. There's a couple of job agencies in town, I used one once before, years ago, got an afternoon's washing up in a care home within a few minutes of walking in the front door of the agency. I imagine a similar scenario now, staff grateful that I've come in, whisking me away to an immediate start, a desperate employer lucky to have me on board. It's all my imagination though, I don't even get to sit down in there, I'm still standing at the open front door and they're telling me they only want skilled professionals. Things have changed, mostly jobs that need specific qualifications, long term clerical posts, they don't have anything temporary.

At the local job centre I ask where they post the vacancies, I remember the wall of hand written cards you used to be able to look along. They say they don't do that any more, there's no jobs at the job centre, you have to look on their website. So I end up back at a computer screen cobbling together a CV, trying to put a respectable spin on our current lifestyle, overplaying my last proper job.

I follow the maze of searching online, job websites, the Friday Ad, Gumtree, local listings and notice boards. There isn't much but I send off a couple of applications forgetting what they're even for. Maybe I should get back to town, do the rounds and see if I've missed anything.

I've got my jacket on when the phone rings. An upbeat lady from a local insurance company says they have my application, can I come for an interview? They have an office in Eastbourne, the guy that runs the team that are looking for a temp will be in town at the end of the afternoon.

When I get there he's young, boyish with a bony handshake and a bulging briefcase. He suggests we go into town for coffee, already I like how this is going. I've heard you like someone more when you meet them if you have a warm cup of coffee in your hand. We sit in the window of a coffee chain in the Arndale Centre, he goes to the counter and orders two cappuccinos, bringing them back on a tray. His mobile beeps a couple of times, he looks at the screen, places it face down on the table and says to no one or maybe to me,

"I'll deal with that in a minute."

I pick up the warm cup of coffee, cradle it in my hands, he does the same. Then he asks a few casual questions, I manage to account for my current situation, a professional musician in a short hiatus whilst my wife and musical partner recovers from a broken wrist. He's sympathetic, I keep it brief. He says he's in charge of a team that's currently sorting out some problems created by glitches in the computer software. Most customers have come out better off and the company has absorbed the loss. A few have got charged a higher premium so these ones are getting a refund. Anyway, the job is to find out which is which, correct the errors and they need an extra person to get it done quicker.

His phone beeps again, he ignores it to

sip more coffee then checks his list of interview questions. His eyes skim down the page, darting from left to right, he's missing some of them off. I think he's missing most of them off, I'm grateful he doesn't ask me where I see myself in five years time. I don't even know where I'll be in five weeks time.

I refer to jobs I've done that sound respectable, emphasising my ease with computers. Why do we still say that? Even octogenarians have iPads and are banking and shopping online. It seems to elicit the right kind of reaction though. I leave space so he can fill the gaps with the thought that hiring me is the answer, another problem solved for him and he can get on and reply to the messages piling up on his phone. We take our last lukewarm mouthful of coffee, put the empty cups back on the tray. He says he wouldn't normally tell the applicant if they've got the job until he gets back to the office but on this occasion he can tell me now, I'm in. Eight weeks of work in an office. It's Thursday,

"Can I start tomorrow?"

He suggests next Monday.

So there I am the following week in an ironed shirt and smart trousers, getting a corporate induction to the firm. Filling out forms for HR and payroll, a quick tour of the building, the canteen and rest areas before I'm handed over to my team on the third floor. There's four of us. Rebecca, Emily and Steve came in a couple of weeks ago from different departments to get this task done, they say our line manager, the guy who interviewed me, isn't here much.

Rebecca is the friendliest, kind, a young mum, she has two little kids and brings the role into work as well. I'm grateful for that. Emily is friendly too, she's younger, she can't be that many years out of school. Distracted, talkative, busy with a social life in and out of work. Any reason to get out of her chair and go somewhere else in the building and she takes it and will be gone for ages. She knows someone on every floor, she's popular and gets away with it, bluffing her way out of it anytime she's asked where she's been. When she's in her seat she likes to talk, always something to catch up on, boyfriends, girlfriends, family, haircuts, weekends and holidays.

Steve is the opposite, quiet, a concentrated look in his face, tall and thin with blonde hair, probably in his twenties. I can tell he doesn't want to be here and doesn't say a lot, too much communication might strengthen the chains that are binding him here. On the first day I take his lead when he starts getting ready to leave in the minutes leading up to 5pm. His jacket's on and buttoned up, his bag's on the desk. Poised on the edge of his seat he flies out the door on the hour, not a second later. I'm not far behind him and neither is anyone else that finishes at five, we're all streaming down the stairwells, gushing out into the fresh air like we've been submerged underwater too long. Up ahead at the front of the crowd I can see Steve, his long legs powering him away, putting the distance between him and the day job before disappearing out of view.

In the office we all sit in a line, the four of us in one row, my desk furthest from the window. I'm not able to see out of it and I'm glad, I don't want to start daydreaming, thinking too much, wondering what the hell I'm doing here on this side of the glass. How I ended up tapping away at a computer keyboard in an ironed shirt and smart trousers.

There's around eight other teams in our large office. Six or more people in each team, sat around their own array of tables. To my left are a group of supervisors taking queries from staff on another floor. They're the only people in this room on the phone and their loud voices carry. Answering queries from agents in other offices who are on the phone to customers, problems they can't answer, needing advice. I can hear the advice, every word of it, everyone can,

"'Allo mate."

The loudest voice of them all, a big guy that starts every call like this with any agent he knows and he knows a lot of them. Then he talks through the situation, gives his advice, the resolution, the closing of the call, a minute will pass and then,

"'Allo mate."

Those two words lengthened out, taking longer than they should. At least I'm listening to the solution, it could be worse, I could be listening to the question, never knowing the answer.

At the table behind me are a group of large women working through manual correspondence.

They're also working through a large tub of Haribo sweets, when the tub is nearly empty one of them volunteers to pick another one up on their way in the next day. Their work station's like a scene in a Beryl Cook painting, ladies opening letters, chatting, typing, reaching over with arms outstretched, fingers fumbling in a giant jar taking handfuls of brightly coloured candy.

None of the teams really talk to each other. In an open plan office it's like there are invisible walls surrounding each nest of tables. When our line manager eventually stops by to check in on the team, I remember the good chat we had over coffee last week, our informal interview. I want to give him an "'allo mate", but he's less friendly, looking in my direction with only slight acknowledgement. The gap between us has widened, the hierarchy of the workplace has asserted itself. Moody fried egg.

Jayne's started gentle physio on the fingers of her left hand. No one said anything about her not being able to play again, we're hoping and praying that she can. Nobody gave us doomsday scenarios but maybe because they were in French and we didn't understand what they were saying.

Most evenings Jayne and I walk down to the seafront. That little wrist seems so delicate, I have to try to put it out of my mind when we're out together, all the uneven surfaces, crooked pavements and kerbs. Through the town centre, past the homeless people in shop doorways. Impossible not to question our situation, how we got here, the big question of what we're doing, why we did it all in the first place?

Jayne gets a call from Dervla. The only thing that was in the diary, going to Ireland, has just fallen through. She's not well enough, she needs an operation and has to postpone indefinitely. What are we going to do now? Walking along the promenade at night, looking out at the sea, the uncertainty and our problems, the wind in our faces, hoping it'll blow them all away. The front half of Eastbourne pier is a burnt skeleton, standing like the body of a dinosaur on the beach, it's black frame all that remains after it caught fire and was destroyed a couple of months ago.

On a Saturday night our wing mirror gets smashed by a drunken passer by, there's a police notice on the van asking us to call the station. A neighbour heard the disturbance, saw it happen and reported it, other vehicles got damaged too. They might need a statement to help convict the guy they caught. In the end they don't need anything from us and apologise there isn't any compensation. £20 to repair it, not a big deal, just a thing that can be replaced. Maybe it's saying more than that, a broken wing mirror telling us to stop looking back, stop reflecting. What's gone is gone, what's done is done.

I ring Martini Bob, see how he's doing,

"Hey Bob, we're thinking of selling that speaker we left with you."

"Err, that's the thing see, it's been such a long time."

He was having a clear out and gave it to a

friend a while ago,

"Sorry about that."

"No problem Bob."

What's gone is gone, what's done is done, look at the road ahead. We speak to Shinina, arrange a date to go and collect our mail, she says we need to start looking for somewhere else to send our mail, they're putting their house on the market, looking at buying somewhere cheap in Bulgaria, going to live there.

I go with Jayne to her appointment at the local hospital. There's a lot of people waiting in the queue, so many other broken limbs. Arms, wrists, legs and ankles, people sat in chairs along the corridor in slings, plaster casts, bandages, crutches leaning against the wall. This place is busy, mending a lot of collisions with hard surfaces, all those bumps, crashes, trips and falls. The consultant is curious to see how the French have put the pins in, he says everyone does it differently and they can take the pins out in a few weeks.

When the pins come out where will we go? I'm being paid weekly, putting as much away as I can. Now that Ireland isn't happening I ask at work if I can carry on a bit longer, they say they can use me for two more weeks. Jayne's on the case, typing with one hand, looking for a house sit, looking for the next chapter in our life, it seems shrouded in mist.

12. THE END OR THE BEGINNING?

"**H**ow about going to Ramsgate?"

Jayne's asking but she already knows the answer. I can tell it's already sorted and there's a plan. She's just had the pins in her wrist out, it's still delicate but the physio she's doing every day means there's more movement. Being able to pick up a pair of socks is a big deal.

"It's a house sit, another Irish writer and author."

She's going to Spain and needs someone to look after her house and cats for two months. Sounds good, I could get another temp job, we might start to make sense of our future. If Jayne's wrist keeps improving, who knows, we could even start looking at booking gigs.

I've only been working for ten weeks but the team at the office get me a farewell card. They've all written something inside, mostly drawing smiley faces, signing their names and wishing me good luck. For once I feel I need it, I don't have much to say about our plans when they ask what's next. My mum has a concerned look in her eyes as well, wishing us luck as I drive us to Ramsgate.

Our host lives in a little terraced house in the backstreets. Narrow roads, cars parked bumper to bumper on both sides, just enough room to squeeze the van between them.

Tara answers the door, treats us like long lost relatives, her soft southern Irish accent welcoming, generous, making a fuss of us. Warm and reassuring like she could deliver bad news and you wouldn't notice. Tara Moore, she's a writer, a published novelist, when I take our bags up to our room there's a poster of one of her books on the wall beside the staircase.

"Help yourselves to anything and I'll see you in a couple of months."

And then she's gone and it's just us and the two cats. Lizzie and Capone, as in Al Capone. If he was human we soon realise he'd probably end up in prison too. He's big, bullish and hungry, his unopened sachets of food high up on a shelf often have claw marks in them from where he's attempted to get them himself. At night we have to wrap the duvet completely around our feet otherwise he makes a sport of attacking them, paws swiping under the covers at the bottom of the bed. We help him let off steam by tying a cotton reel to a long piece of string, swinging it along the hallway whilst standing overhead on the stairs, once or twice a day keeps him more chilled overnight.

Lizzie on the other hand is a bony little

skeleton covered in fur, wants to sit on you no matter what's going on. When I'm playing guitar she jumps on my knees, I have to hold them together so there's enough of a platform for her to curl up and sleep. Or if I'm at the computer she'll want to coil up on the keyboard. I scoop her off, fingers gently separating fur and bone from each of the keys until she's lying in my outstretched hand. She doesn't mind though, as long as prising her off means she ends up on my lap. Like a little Russian hat, a furry bundle of heat that you could put on your head for winter warmth.

I go to look for a job in the first few days. The only thing I come across in town is a sign outside an amusement arcade, a hand written notice in the blacked out window says they have a job vacancy. I go in, it's empty of people, dimly lit apart from the flashing lights of fruit machines and the promise of jackpots. The woman behind the security screen says the boss isn't there and to come back later. I decide not to.

There's a venue in town, Ramsgate Music Hall, we go to listen to a band and get talking to a woman working on the door. Jo, petite with high cheekbones and eyebrows, like a pixie, black hair up in a pony tale. She works at a cafe as well, on Sundays they have an open mic in the afternoon, says we should go along. The place is called Vinyl Head.

Jayne's playing ukulele again, going easy on her wrist. She can hold chords down now and everyday we go through songs, each day she plays more of them for longer until a few Sunday's later and she says she's ready. We put our instruments in their cases and walk the short distance to another backstreet of Ramsgate.

"Hello my darlings, come in, come in."

The owner greets us like he's been waiting for us all day. Seeing our instrument cases and that we've come along to play at the open mic he immediately offers us coffee. Behind the counter are two record players, he lifts the needle of one of them, swiftly, delicately placing a new vinyl on the turntable before making our drinks. Pressurised steam from the coffee machine obscures the first bars of the music and then I can hear it, The Velvet Underground. The music matches the decor, the psychedelic swinging sixties, a primary colour scheme. There's a red sofa in the shape of a pair of lips, a monster movie sci-fi poster, a Hofner bass guitar hanging on the wall, like the one Paul McCartney uses.

Humberto, Humbi, hands us our two coffees. He's from Spain, a round face, his short hair a mirror image of his short dark beard. I can tell he loves his cafe, not only that but he loves the people that come in it. Everyone coming through the door gets a "hello my darling" or a big "hi", he knows all their names.

By the display of vinyls all around the walls his biggest passion is music, a passion and enthusiasm that spills out in his language, flamboyant phrases like "so gorgeous" and "wonderful", where the 'r' gets an extra roll from his Spanish tongue. Somehow between talking and him serving and greeting customers, he's changing the records on the decks, keeping track of the mood, effortlessly switching vinyls.

When it's time for us to play a few songs he gently fades the volume out. At most gigs when it comes to turning off the house music it's just switched straight off, the abruptness jolts people like there's been a power cut, then all eyes turn to the musicians as if to say,

"So you're the reason they had to turn the music off."

Humbi is more sensitive to the music and the environment than this and fades a chilled vibe back in gently when we finish. We get a "so gorgeous" and a "wonderful" and he offers us more drinks,

"Why don't you come and play a concert next Saturday?"

He says they'll advertise it, pass the hat round during the performance to pay us something. We have our first gig.

Vinyl Head turns out to be a hub for local artists and musicians. Humbi attracts a creative crowd, at the gig the following Saturday we get suggestions about where to play around the area.

With some leads we get straight on the case with emails and phone calls. Before long we've arranged a self styled 'World Tour of Thanet', finishing back at our favourite cafe in town. A chance for me to drive us out to some local venues, get our act together, play and earn some money. We're getting there, Jayne's getting there, she can play on most of the songs now.

Time to look further afield as Tara's coming back soon. Any gig around the country we can think of from last year or the year before, repeats, new leads, anything, everything. Dots in the diary haphazardly join together.

I glance behind me into the back of the van. There they are, all our worldly possessions, packed away and in their place. Sure, we could still do with getting rid of some stuff but the bed is clear, just a couple of things to move off it when it comes to getting ready for sleep. Jayne is flexing her left hand in the driver's seat, opening and closing her fingers, palm facing her like they're having a silent and meaningful dialogue.

"Are you sure you're ready?"

She looks at me, nods, there's no doubt in her mind, her right hand turns the key in the ignition. I wind the window down, the noise of the engine becomes louder, a steady purring rhythm. Jayne slowly turns the wheel, edges us out of the parking space, then we're moving, rolling down the road in our little ship on wheels. Closing the window, the space around us becomes quieter. The captain is back at the helm and we're sailing again. Sailing into the unknown, out into a sea of uncertainty, all it's randomness, strangeness and beauty. I look at Jayne, she's at home behind the wheel, sitting upright in her seat, ready to start over, ready for anything. She senses I'm watching her, her face creases into a smile and she turns her head until our eyes meet. I'm thinking it, but she says it,

"Here we go again."

Have you come this far with us? Big thanks if you have. Please feel free to leave a review and let others know about this book. You might also like to come and see us play live if we're anywhere in your area. For more information including gig dates, albums and videos you can visit our website wildwoodjack.com

THANKS

Thanks to Tara Moore for her enthusiasm and positivity when I first showed her the rough beginning of this book. It meant such a lot to me to have that encouragement from the start. Also to Jayne for her endless reading and re-reading of all the drafts and changes. Thanks to Tom Fairnie for taking a read through and giving feedback.

Our journey on the road wouldn't be what it is without mentioning and thanking a few other people too, many of whom came into our lives in the years following the timescale in this book :

Simon Parkin for the great cover design, Lis & Pete, Stella, Paul & Aileen, Will & Vanessa, Humbi, Fiz & David, Sophie & Julie Brown, Jilly, Caroline & Ken, Tim (for being a great friend and the long term use of his barn through all the lockdowns), Shinina & Carlos, Bob Thrussell, Sue & David in Loro Piceno, Adrian & Siggi, John & Ros Butcher, Kat & Mat, Ian and Sheryl, Gillian & Arthur, Jackie Gibson, Julia and Shaun, Jeff & Chanel, Jae & Rob, Andrew & Kirsten London, Brenda & Mark, Val & John, Harvey Summers, Steve & Tina Hart, Janet Vahl, Rupi & Kati, Mark & Marion, Rosie & Steve, Tom & Jane Fairnie, Sheila Turner, Caroline & Peter Jones, Pete

Boddis, Helge Engelbrecht, Mike & Jan Hopkins, Joni & Bruce, David Gray & Gill, Helen Hill, Jane & John Walton, Richard & Knitting Ann, Nick & Keith at the New Forest Folk Festival, Tommy Kristensen, Ness and all the other people who've shown us kindness, support and friendship on our way.

ABOUT THE AUTHOR

Adam Piggott

Adam was born in Brighton in 1969 and grew up in Eastbourne. He studied at Thames, Bath and Hull University where he met Jayne in 1991.

After graduating with qualifications he didn't know what to do with he became a circus juggler for two years. Jayne and Adam began playing gigs in various bands from 2007 before setting out on their own songwriting journey in 2010. As of 2022 they are still on the road and performing as the duo Wildwood Jack.

Printed in Great Britain
by Amazon